PATRICIA M. FERGUS
University of Minnesota

D1464253

SPELLING IMPROVEMENT

A PROGRAM FOR SELF-INSTRUCTION
THIRD EDITION

McGraw-Hill Book Company

New York   St. Louis   San Francisco   Auckland   Bogotá
Düsseldorf   Johannesburg   London   Madrid   Mexico   Montreal
New Delhi   Panama   Paris   São Paulo   Singapore   Sydney
Tokyo   Toronto

SPELLING
IMPROVEMENT
A PROGRAM FOR
SELF-INSTRUCTION

67890 FGRFGR 8321

This book was set in News Gothic by
Monotype Composition Company, Inc.
The editors were Donald W. Burden and James R. Belser;
the cover was designed by Anne Canevari Green;
the production supervisor was Donna Piligra.
Fairfield Graphics was printer and binder.

Library of Congress Cataloging in Publication Data

Fergus, Patricia M
  Spelling improvement.

  Includes index.
  1. English language—Orthography and spelling.
2. Vocabulary. I. Title.
PE1143.F4 1978   428'.1   77-21675
ISBN 0-07-020456-X

Contents

Preface

The third edition, like its predecessors, places prime importance on spelling as a multisensory process and as an integral part of written communication. It has the same objective: to help those who misspell words for a variety of reasons to improve their spelling; and the same audience: those who can read and understand high school texts. It also has the same flexibility for adoption: to be used in courses or independent study in high schools, colleges and universities, and technical and trade schools; in educational programs in business, industry, and government; or independently by those motivated to increase their spelling power.

Since the publication of the second edition, it has become increasingly apparent that a comprehensive yet short diagnostic test, easy to administer and analyze, would add immeasurably to the text. From this single addition evolved a full-scale testing program: diagnostic test; chapter pretests, reviews, and posttests; tests for Parts One, Two, and Three, and a final test. A growing interest in the development of the English language has also become apparent. To help stimulate this interest "The English Writing System" section in the Introduction includes more etymological references, and Chapter 2 discusses the Latin prefix *ad* and the process of assimilation. Also in the Introduction a new section, "Features of the Book," presents distinctive aspects of the text, and an expanded section, "To the Student," gives concrete suggestions for its use.

Retained from the previous edition are the format; the content; and the emphasis on syllabication as a method for good spelling, on critical points in words, and on spelling of words in context and in isolation, the latter required for accurate proofreading of one's writing. Inasmuch as the content has not been changed, the gratifying results of the testing of the second edition prior to publication apply also to this edition. The added tests have been administered to numerous college students and refined wherever necessary.

In preparing this revision I am reminded of my in-debtedness to the reviewers who painstakingly read the previous editions and to the many students who studied the text, took the tests, and offered cogent comments about both.

Patricia M. Fergus

SPELLING IMPROVEMENT
A PROGRAM FOR SELF-INSTRUCTION

Introduction

THE ENGLISH WRITING SYSTEM

A writing system develops chiefly from attempts to standardize and innovate and from the political and educational
movements rather than from the linguistic process itself.
The English language has had an interesting development.
It was introduced in its earliest form from about the
middle of the fifth century by the Angles, Saxons, and
tribes from the northern part of Germany. These invaders
eventually founded kingdoms of their own, and from the
language of these Teutonic settlers developed the national
tongue. This Anglo-Saxon period, usually called "the Old
English period," extended until about 1100, when "the
Middle English period" began and which continued until
1500.

Of the three English periods—Old, Middle, and Modern
—the Middle period had the most effect on the writing
system as we know it today. There were gradual changes
in spelling to correspond better with various sounds.
There were sometimes several different developments of
phonemes which produced striking inconsistencies in modern English spelling, one of the most interesting yet
plaguing being gh (*through, rough, caught*).

From the twelfth century until well into the fourteenth,
many who wrote in English were extremely proficient in
French and brought many of the aspects of the French
language into English. For example, they borrowed the
French *ou* to replace the English *u* (as in *house* or *found*);
they borrowed whole words from the French; and they re-
placed many English characters with those from the
French.

Greek words were also borrowed during this period, and

although the Greek alphabet was related historically to the Latin alphabet, it was different enough to cause some problems. The Greek letters had to be represented by Roman letters, and in this representation decisions had to be made about the original or altered pronunciation and spelling. The familiar silent *p* at the beginning of such words as *psychology* and *pneumonia* or the "f" sound of *ph* in *philosophy* and *sophomore* can be linked to this period of borrowing from the Greek.

In the latter part of the Middle English period Latin loan words remained virtually unchanged, resulting in the addition of more rules to those already in use from Old English and French. An interesting point concerning Latin and French during this period of development is the spelling of several English suffixes. *Able* and *ible,* which often cause spelling difficulties today, were the French spellings from the Latin *abilis* or *ibilis,* the choice of which depended on the stem vowel of the Latin verb. Two other suffixes, *ance* and *ence,* are derived from the Latin verb endings *antem* and *entem,* but they have no relationship to phonological or grammatical systems of English today. Not only do we have problems with suffixes, but we also have silent letters which have either carried over from the Old English period or which were put back into words like *doubt* and *debt* by scholars who wanted the Latin derivation to be apparent.

The period generally from about 1350 to 1550 is considered the transition from Middle to Modern English, and it is in this stage that we have the Great Vowel Shift. Here the long stressed vowels moved forward in the mouth; for example, the *i* which was pronounced as a long e became the I that we know today as the personal pronoun. It was also at this time that the printing houses (printing having been brought into England by William Caxton in the midst of the shift) endeavored to standardize the spelling of many words and conventions, such as the initial and medial use of *i,* the final use of *y,* and the reduction of double consonants, but at the same time tended to retain some of the Middle English spelling. What resulted is obvious today: Some of our biggest problems in spelling are due to the variance between pronunciation and graphic presentation.

A few examples will illustrate this variance. Consider *sword* and *two*—the *w,* which earlier represented a semivowel, has ceased to be pronounced, but the letter remains. Or consider *climb* and *dumb*—the *b* is not pronounced, yet the letter remains. The final e has varied from period to period, sometimes sounding like an unstressed vowel, sometimes not sounding, appearing at the end of a word because of a printer's whim to fill out a line. Today the diacritic e in the final position, although not pronounced, has specific functions: (a) to make the preceding vowel long (tōne, cāke, dīke); (b) to help produce the "v" sound in words like stove or nave; (c) to indicate a final "s" sound (peace) or a final "z" sound (muse).

Linguistic research has shown that a greater proportion of the English language is more phonetic than we realize and that spelling patterns are often predictable. For instance, the "s" sound is usually written s at the beginning (say) but ss at the end (mess). The "k" sound at the beginning, if followed by i or e, is spelled k (kill, kennel); if followed by a, o, u, it is spelled c (card, cope, custard). In the final position the "k" sound may be spelled ck in a stressed syllable (back, neck) but c in an unstressed syllable (traf'fic, chron'ic).

Because the language is quite phonetic and patterns are often predictable, we can spell correctly. True, some words may perplex us for a while, but with so many helpful guides we should not misspell any words for long.

REASONS FOR POOR SPELLING

One reason, touched on in the previous section, has to do with the words themselves. There are silent letters that must be included in the graphic presentation; there are suffixes that sound alike (able-ible, ary-ery, ance-ence) which must be selected for appropriate root words; there are vowels with slight or hardly any stress that must be correctly identified. There are also complete words that sound exactly alike (homonyms), so they must be distinguished by their meanings. For instance, the sets cite-site-sight and principal-principle have a single pronunciation but many meanings, and it is these definitions that tell us which to choose.

Another reason is that we do not pronounce words clearly and distinctly. We may add or omit syllables; we may slur vowels or consonants or even syllables. Although many of us have two patterns of oral expression (formal and informal), the choice depending upon circumstances, we must remember that written expression does not offer much choice. Dr. Samuel Johnson, author of the Dictionary of the English Language (1755) aptly described the problem of two pronunciations, one colloquial and cursory, the other regular and solemn: "The cursory pronunciation is always vague and uncertain, being made different in different mouths by negligence, unskilfulness, or affectation. The solemn pronunciation, though by no

means immutable and permanent, is yet always less re-
mote from the orthography, and less liable to capricious
innovation." We may talk to a close friend about the failings of 'goverment,' but if we write to the mayor, we had
better discuss the failings of *government.*

Lastly, some words have characteristic ways of retaining or dropping the final letter before adding a suffix,
forming the plural or possessive, or being spelled *ie* or *ei.*
By learning a few uncomplicated rules and applying them
to a goodly number of words, we can increase our spelling
efficiency.

NEED FOR CORRECT SPELLING

The answer to the question posed by some students, "Why
should I bother to spell correctly?" is obvious in the number of marked-up high school themes, college term papers,
reports, and even theses and dissertations; in the number
of applications turned down by prospective employers;
and in the promotions that fail to materialize. But the most
important reason is often overlooked or ignored: clear
communication. When we write, we attempt to set forth
our ideas intelligibly and accurately for someone else to
read. And even though the reader may detect these ideas,
he or she can be disconcerted and irked by misspelled
words interrupting the continuity and flow. The result?
Alienation of the reader, something no writer can afford.

PURPOSE OF THE BOOK

This text is designed to help individuals who misspell
words for a variety of reasons to *improve* their spelling.
Inasmuch as the primary emphases are on pronunciation,
meaning of words, and syllabication, the chapters have
been grouped together into three parts: One—Sound and
Spelling; Two—Meaning and Spelling; Three—Rules and
Spelling. Part One concentrates on the sound difficulties
of the words themselves and on the problems of correct
pronunciation and enunciation. Part Two emphasizes the
words whose meaning determines both choice and spelling. Part Three stresses some simple rules for words
ending in final e, final y, plurals, and the like. Although
the word "rules" may set up an initially adverse reaction,
the few given in this text will form the basis for spelling a
great number of words correctly.

Research has proved that good spellers have a method,

and because that method usually consists of dividing words into parts, a unit entitled Guidelines for Syllabication appears at the conclusion of the program. This concise presentation will provide sufficient tools to divide not only the words in the book but also words encountered in the future.

The book is not a panacea for all spelling ills, but for those who misspell words like *beginning, desirous,* or *loneliness,* it offers concrete help to overcome such difficulties. It also furnishes a solid basis for independent study by making students aware that spelling is a multisensory process and that pronunciation and sound, etymology and sound, meaning, and syllabication play important roles in good spelling.

It is hoped that the etymological references throughout will stimulate students' curiosity and motivate them to study word origins and their effect on spelling.

FEATURES OF THE BOOK

Through the technique of programming, students, at their own pace, apply what they learn by spelling correctly a large number of words in the program plus other words presenting similar problems. Special features are:

1. The text is a unified instructional system, and owing to the sixteen self-contained chapter units and an appendix on syllabication, it has an inherent flexibility—students can study the whole program or particular sections only.

2. Reasons for misspelling are emphasized throughout, with students becoming aware (perhaps for the first time) of the roles that sound, word origin, and meaning play in the spelling process.

3. Each chapter introduction presents behavioral objectives so that students know exactly what they are to accomplish by the end of the chapter.

4. Built into the text is a complete testing program. A diagnostic test pinpoints problems, or potential problems; chapter pretests offer a more detailed diagnosis and a basis for comparison with the posttests; reviews, strategically placed for completion of short learning units, allow for immediate testing; chapter posttests indicate immediate progress; tests for Parts One, Two, and Three provide further (and delayed) indication of progress; a final test shows the overall accomplishment. Answers for all tests are in Appendix B.

5. After the answers for each pretest and posttest students will find frame references for incorrect answers so that they can review the corresponding frames or sections.

6. Most of the words in the program appear in numerous lists of words commonly misspelled by high school and college students and by adults in business. Inasmuch as a number are defined and presented in context, the program builds vocabulary and improves spelling. Of especial importance are the references to the origin of words; these can increase students' knowledge of the English language and also pique their curiosity about language in general.

TO THE STUDENT

1. *Using the text.*
a. If you have not already done so, read the Preface and the Introduction for a brief overview.
b. Complete the diagnostic test (read the introductory and explanatory remarks and directions carefully).
c. Take the short pretest in Appendix A. Your score will determine whether you complete this unit or bypass it.
d. Proceed to the program. Wherever you start, take the chapter pretest—if you have ninety percent of the answers correct, you may bypass the chapter. If you work the chapter, complete the posttest to note improvement. The chapters have several reviews, so you may wait one or two days or longer before taking the posttest. Whether you bypass any chapters or not, complete the Part tests and the final examination—you may also delay these tests for a better indication of your progress and final accomplishment.
e. For immediate and complete references for any word(s) you misspell, check the listing of answer numbers and corresponding frames after each pretest and posttest.

2. *Responding.* As one frame is dependent on another for understanding and continuity, you should work carefully and at times slowly. In other words, you must apply what you learn. Several types of frames require different responses, such as filling in letters; discriminating between groups of words; writing of single words, parts of words, or a phrase or two. Even though you can answer some frames quickly with just mental responses, it is better to write the words and "feel" them.

Each frame is numbered and may require more than one response. If dotted lines appear in a frame, write your answer(s) for questions up to those lines and check to see if you are correct—then go to the next part of the same frame. If a frame requires more than one response and does *not* have dotted lines, answer *all* parts and then check.

If you have a wrong answer, reread the frame. Do not hesitate about going back over a frame or two—there is no penalty for rereading. If you miss a question or two (or parts of a question) in a review, return to the beginning of that particular unit or to the specific frames pertinent to the wrong answer, and refresh your memory. It may be necessary to reread only a few frames for a better start.

Because the answers are immediately available, it is possible to cheat. Eyes that wander will not improve your spelling, so cover the answer side of the page with a small card (a 3 by 5 will do), sliding it down as you check the answer(s) to one frame but not revealing the answer(s) for the next frame.

3. *Timing.* Each chapter is divided into short units of material with a review for each unit. If time prevents you from finishing a chapter, stop after a review so as not to break the continuity. Otherwise, you may be forced to try picking up where you left off or to return to the beginning and reread.

Because this is programmed material, work as rapidly or as slowly as you wish or as the material demands.

All frames are not the same length, so do not anticipate finishing the same number in the same length of time. Some requiring discrimination and application take longer than others requiring a letter or a single word.

If you do not know the meaning of a word in the introductory or explanatory material, consult the dictionary. The "dictionary habit" is a must for good spelling, good writing, and good reading.

Diagnostic Test

INTRODUCTION

Proofreading an original composition is undoubtedly the ultimate test of spelling efficiency. Inasmuch as accurate proofreading entails reading words, not necessarily whole thoughts, a list of correctly and incorrectly spelled words can serve as a diagnostic indicator. But remember this: the diagnostic test is simply that, nothing more. There are no passing scores, no levels to attain; there are just words to spell so that existing or potential difficulties can be identified, treated, and cured.

To provide maximum coverage of principles within a minimum of space and time, the test has two sections: the first for Parts One and Two, the second for Part Three. Neither section is long, so you may wish to complete both at one sitting and be prepared to start from the beginning of the book or at a particular chapter. Or you may prefer to complete Section A and go on to Parts One and Two, then Section B and on to Part Three.

The best way to take the test is to work quickly and conscientiously. Do not guess or hesitate unduly. Puzzling over any part of a given word means you do not have that word at your fingertips. The test must show all the words you consistently misspell or are apt to misspell.

DIRECTIONS:

If the word is spelled *correctly*, write C (for correct) in the blank. If the word is *misspelled, write it correctly*. If you do *not know* the correct spelling, write U (for unknown).

SECTION A

1. mischievious   _____
2. discriptive   _____
3. accumulate   _____
4. exhaustive   _____
5. catagory   _____
6. surprize   _____
7. admissible   _____
8. preceed   _____
9. principal (rule)   _____
10. loose (to misplace)   _____
11. government   _____
12. perspire   _____
13. intrest   _____
14. rythm   _____
15. dormatory   _____
16. experience   _____
17. expressable   _____
18. superseded   _____
19. compliment (to praise)   _____
20. effect (result)   _____
21. atheletics   _____
22. unecessary   _____
23. loneliness   _____
24. gardian   _____
25. definate   _____
26. insistent   _____
27. horrible   _____
28. procede   _____
29. its' (poss. pron.)   _____
30. advise (to counsel)   _____
31. wonderous   _____
32. mistated   _____
33. posession   _____

34. condemning _____

35. similiar _____

36. noticable _____

37. cemetary _____

38. accede _____

39. past (moved on) _____

40. quite (not noisy) _____

41. rememberance _____

42. reccomend _____

43. explaination _____

44. answered _____

45. seperation _____

46. existence _____

47. creditable _____

48. concede _____

49. its (it is) _____

50. affect (to change) _____

51. temperment _____

52. preformed _____

53. aquire _____

54. knelt _____

55. peculiar _____

56. defendent _____

57. analize _____

58. antecedent _____

59. to (in excess) _____

60. causal (unconcerned) _____

SECTION B

1. equiped _____

2. benefitting _____

3. nineth _____

4. desireous _____

5. attorneys _____

6. feign _____

7. vetos _____

8. boy's (poss.—one) _____

9. wholy _____

10. adventureous _____

11. begining _____

12. panicked _____

13. becomeing _____

14. writting _____

15. accompanying _____

16. sieze _____

17. copys _____

18. ours' (poss. pron.) _____

19. drasticly _____

20. advantagous _____

21. preference _____

22. tonage _____

23. singeing (burning) _____

24. immensity _____

25. studing _____

26. freindship _____

27. calfs _____

28. churches' (poss.—several) _____

29. basically _____

30. piteous _____

31. omited _____

32. occurence _____

33. ninty _____

34. receivable _____

35. batteries _____

36. deceitful _____

37. thiefs _____

38. father-in-law's (poss.—one) _____

39. practicaly _____

40. mountainous   _____

41. referral   _____

42. confering   _____

43. denseity   _____

44. changing   _____

45. trys   _____

46. besiege   _____

47. echos   _____

48. womens' (poss.—several)   _____

49. lonly   _____

50. courageous   _____

51. rebelling   _____

52. equippage   _____

53. oweing   _____

54. changeable   _____

55. pityful   _____

56. anceint   _____

57. potatoe   _____

58. her's (poss. pron.)   _____

59. hungrily   _____

60. spaceous   _____

CORRECTING AND ANALYZING THE DIAGNOSTIC TEST

This test has been devised to give you an item-by-item analysis of spelling problems covered in the text. Section A has sixty items and includes problems in Chapters 1 through 9. Section B also has sixty items, and includes problems in Chapters 10 through 16.

In each section, items ending with the *same number* pertain to a specific problem. Take Section A for example. All 1s (*1, 11, 21, 31, 41, 51*) relate to Pronunciation and Enunciation, Chapter 1; all 2s (*2, 12, 22, 32, 42, 52*) relate to Prefixes, Chapter 2; and so on. Because there are a number of *suffixes* that cause spelling difficulties, twice as many words have been included for a more accurate diagnosis. You will see when correcting your test that items ending in 6 and 7 relate to Sound-alike Suffixes, Chapter 6.

Section B is set up the same way: items ending in the *same number* apply to a specific problem. And for certain problems you will find twice as many words: items ending in 1 and 2 pertain to Doubling the Final Consonant, Chapter 10; items ending in 3 and 4 to Final *E*, Chapter 11.

Now you are ready to correct your test.

1. Turn to the answer key in Appendix B and check all *incorrect* answers (*C*'s that are wrong, words that are spelled incorrectly, and all *U*'s).

2. *Total* the *incorrect* answers in each section. This will give you a general idea of your spelling performance. For instance, if you missed 10 out of 60 you had 16% incorrect; 25 out of 60, 42%; 30 out of 60, 50%; and so forth.

3. In both sections count the *incorrect* answers for *each* item (all 1s, then all 2s, 3s through 0s). In Section A be sure to add 6 and 7 and in Section B add 1 and 2, and 3 and 4. Below is a sample tally—use it as a guide for correcting your test.

DIAGNOSTIC TEST ——— Student *X* ————

SECTION A

ITEM	CHAPTER TITLE	TALLY	TOTAL
1.	Pronunciation and Enunciation	7++/	5
2.	Prefixes		0
3.	Syllabication	7++/	5
4.	Silent Letters	///	3
5.	Vowel Stress	////	4
6.	Sound-alike Suffixes	// }	5
7.	Sound-alike Suffixes	/// }	
8.	Seed Roots	//	2
9.	Homonyms	/	1
10.	Similar Words	////	4

29

SECTION B

1.	Doubling the Final Consonant	/	
2.	Doubling the Final Consonant	////	5
3.	Final *E*	////	
4.	Final *E*	/////	9
5.	Final Y	////	4
6.	*IE-EI*	//	2
7.	Plurals	///	3
8.	Possessives	/	1
9.	*LY*		0
10.	*OUS*	/	1

25

You now have an item-by-item analysis of your diagnostic test, but what does it mean? Depending on the number of errors, it shows the kinds of spelling problems you *have* or *may have.* For a better understanding, let us refer to the results of Student *X*'s test. There are no errors in Prefixes and *LY* and only 1 apiece in Homonyms, Possessives, and *OUS*. The greatest number is in Final *E* (9), Pronunciation and Enunciation (5) Syllabication (5), Sound-alike Suffixes (5), and Doubling the Final Consonant (5). The rest of the categories have 4 or fewer errors.

Because there are only 6 words for most problems, missing 5 out of 6 amounts to 83% incorrect answers, and constitutes a major difficulty. Even 3 out of 6, or 50% incorrect answers, indicates a major concern. For those items with double the words, missing 9 out of 12, or 75% incorrect, constitutes a major difficulty; missing even 5 out of 12, or 42% incorrect, is cause for concern. To put it another way, you do not want *any* misspellings, so whether you have major or minor problems, you should strive to overcome all of them.

Your spelling problems diagnosed, it is time to begin the program. First take the short pretest in Appendix A (Guidelines for Syllabication) to determine whether you should bypass or work through the section itself, and then go on to any one of the following procedures:
1. Begin with the chapter for which you have the greatest

number of errors, and continue with the next greatest, and on down to the least. As an illustration, Student X would start with Chapter 11, Final E (9 errors), proceed to any one of four chapters for which he (or she) had 5 errors, then to any one of three chapters for which he had 4 errors, ending with Prefixes and LY for which he had none.

2. Begin with Chapter 1 and work straight through the text.

3. For further diagnosis, take the chapter pretests for items with few errors, then choose 1 or 2 above.

4. Devise any system that will give you maximum benefit from the program.

Remember, you *can* improve your spelling!

Part One
SOUND
AND SPELLING

Chapter 1

PRONUNCIATION AND ENUNCIATION

Words can be misspelled because they are not pronounced correctly. Some are mispronounced, with syllables added or omitted; others are not enunciated clearly and distinctly. The words in this chapter have been selected not only for their frequency in being misspelled, but also for their usefulness in illustrating that faulty pronunciation can cause spelling problems. Specific words comprise the material for you to work with, so the objectives for the chapter will be directly concerned with them: to pronounce the words correctly, observing the troublesome spots; to master their spelling; to use them in and out of context; and to encourage you to pronounce and enunciate all words distinctly.

PRETEST

Complete the words below. The definitions will help you to identify them.

1. hin____ance   obstruction
2. rec_og_nize   acknowledge
3. ath_lete_   competitor in sports
4. misch_evic_ous   playful
5. light_en_ing   making lighter
6. trag_edy_   dramatic, disastrous event
7. chim____   passage for smoke and gas
8. temper_ature_   degree of hotness and coldness
9. ath____ics   competitive sports
10. li__ble   responsible for
11. fin____ly   last, at the end
12. dis____trous   calamitous

13. veg_____   edible plant

14. light_____   electrical discharge

15. prej_____   adverse judgment, bias

16. fed_____al   connected with central government

17. remem_____ance   reminder or token

18. griev_____   serious

19. temper_____   disposition

20. quan_____ty   number or amount

21. gov_____ment   process of running political units

22. envi_____ment   surroundings

23. back_____   education, experience

24. gra_____tude   thankfulness

25. hun_____   100

26. ag_____vate   make worse

---

2 3

1. In the first group are words to which an extra syllable is often added. Take *athlete* and *athletics*. You will sometimes hear them pronounced this way: "ath a lete" or "ath a let ics." These are wrong, of course, as *athlete* has just _____ syllables and *athletics* only _____.

ath lete
ath let ics

2. Pronounce the syllables carefully, then write them here: _____ _____ and _____ _____ .

athlete
athletics

3. One who takes part in sports is an _____ and the name for competitive sports is _____ .

2 3

4. Here is another pair: *grievous* and *mischievous*. Often they are pronounced with an extra syllable, but if you say them correctly—griev'ous mis'chievous—you will hear only _____ syllables in *grievous* and _____ in *mischievous*.

griev ous
mis chie vous

5. Pronounce them once more and complete the syllables: griev _____ and mis _____ _____ .

mischievous
grievous

6. It was not a harmful prank, just a mis _____ one.
     The two brothers were responsible for the gr_____ deed.

mischievous
grievous

3

disastrous

disastrous

is not

2
hin   drance

hindrance

remember

no

re   mem   brance

remembrance

3

2

7. The _____ child did not commit a _____ sin.

8. The following words have a common problem. Because they can remind you of a related word, you may include a part of that related word. Take the adjective *disastrous*, which means calamitous. It can remind you of the noun *disaster*, and too often the third syllable (*ter*) is included in the spelling of the adjective "dis as ter ous." *Disastrous*, correctly pronounced and spelled, has how many syllables? _____

9. The results of the election were disas_____.

10. The epidemic of sleeping sickness produced _____ _____ results.

11. Pronounce it once more. There (is, is not) a syllable that sounds like *ter* in this word. _____

12. Like *disastrous*, the word *hindrance* must be pronounced correctly to be spelled correctly. It can remind you of the verb *hinder* (to obstruct), but this reminder can cause you to put an extra syllable in the noun, like "hin der ance." Now pronounce *hindrance*. It has just _____ syllables. What is the second syllable: hin _____.

13. The verb *to hinder* means to obstruct; the noun meaning an obstruction is _____.

14. The noun *remembrance* has the same problem. It can remind you of what verb? _____

15. Pronounce the two words carefully: *remember, remembrance*. Is there a syllable in the noun that sounds liks "ber"? _____
LIKE

16. Divide the word into syllables: _____ _____ _____.

17. My grandmother gave me her gold watch as a re _____.

18. *Remembrance* has only _____ syllables.

19. To be spelled accurately, two other words must also be pronounced correctly: *lightning* and *chimney*. Look at and then pronounce each. Both have _____ syllables.

2

20. Should you pronounce *lightning* with an extra syllable (like "light en ing") you will spell another word, *lightening*, which means becoming lighter. *Lightening* has three syllables. The word you want to spell, defined as an electrical discharge, has how many syllables? _____

lightning

21. Our electric power went out when _____
lightning, lightening
hit the transformer.

lightning

22. Sharp bolts of thunder accompanied the jagged streaks of _____.

chim ney

23. Like *lightning*, the word *chimney* must not have an added syllable. It is not a "chim i ney," but a _____
_____.

chimney

24. The passage through which smoke and gases escape from a furnace is called a smokestack and also a _____
_____.

2

25. The key to spelling *chimney* and *lightning* is to pronounce only _____ syllables in each word.

REVIEW

a. grievous
b. lightning
c. athlete
d. hindrance
e. mischievous
f. remembrance
g. chimney
h. athletics
i. disastrous
j. lightening

26. Now test your skill and fill in the missing letters. The definitions for the words are at the right.

a. griev_____ serious

b. light_____ electrical discharge

c. ath_____ competitor in sports

d. hin_____ obstruction

e. mis_____ playful

f. re_____ reminder or token

g. chim_____ passage for smoke

h. ath_____ competitive sports

i. dis_____ calamitous

j. light_____ becoming lighter

second (the *a*)

27. The second set of words is also an exercise in pronunciation, but it differs from the first in that letters or syllables are omitted, not added. For example, take *liable*, meaning responsible for or likely. It is sometimes pronounced "li ble." But the word is *li a ble*. Which syllable is usually omitted? _____

3

liable

liable

second

fed er al

Federal

federal

third (the *a*)
third (the *a*)
second (the *e*)

vowel

a. temperature
b. temperament
c. vegetable

t

ti

quantity

t

28. The word has how many syllables? _____

29. The word meaning responsible for or likely is _____.

30. Who is _____ for the damages to the car?

31. Like *liable*, the word *federal* causes a problem because the _____ syllable is left out.

32. Like *liable*, the word *federal* has three syllables. Pronounce this word, and then divide it: ____ ____ ____.

33. My uncle has a position with the Fed_____ Communications Commission.

34. Nancy must decide between a job with the state or one with the _____ government.

35. Over the years different pronunciations of words have developed, and occasionally they can cause spelling problems. The words *temperature*, *temperament*, and *vegetable* are good examples. Pronounce each quickly. Each sounds as if it had only three syllables. Which syllable is usually omitted: temperature _____, temperament _____, vegetable _____.

36. In each case you have a syllable in the middle of the word that consists of a single (consonant, vowel). _____

37. Now complete these sentences:

a. The storm caused a severe drop in _____.

b. My cousin Mary Ann has a nervous _____.

c. I don't like a _____ with my meal.

38. The following group of words also has a common problem: if they are not pronounced clearly a letter, in this case a consonant, can be omitted. For example, each syllable in the noun *quantity* must be pronounced distinctly; otherwise what letter can you omit in the second syllable: quan ti ty? _____

39. The second syllable consists of what two letters? _____

40. A number or amount of anything is called _____ _____.

41. In the word that means number or amount, do not forget the consonant _____ in the second syllable.

l

finally

final   ly

n

ern

government

government

beginning

ron

environment

environment

g

42. The adverb *finally* has two parts: the root and the suffix: *final   ly*. When adding *ly* you keep the complete root, so there will be two _____'s in the word.

43. After six hours of debate, the legislature _____ came to an agreement.

44. The word that means at last or at the end consists of the root word _____ and the suffix _____.

45. Like *finally*, the word *government* has a consonant that must be pronounced distinctly; otherwise it may be omitted in the spelling. Pronounce the word by syllables: gov ern ment. Now say it quickly. What consonant in the second syllable can be passed over? _____

46. In other words, it is the second syllable that causes the misspelling: gov _____ ment.

47. My cousin worked sixteen years for the federal _____ _____.

48. The professor then asked, "What form of _____ _____ would be best in this case?"

49. *Environment* has a slightly different problem, but again it is the pronunciation that causes the difficulty. Pronounce the word by syllables: en vi ron ment. Unlike *government* (where the problem is at the end of the second syllable) *environment* has the difficulty at the _____ of the third syllable.

50. Spell this important third syllable: en vi _____ ment.

51. If pollution is not checked in the near future, our _____ will be ruined.

52. An individual can be affected greatly by the _____ _____.

53. The word *background* consists of two words, and although usage has combined them into solid form, both retain their entities as complete words: *back   ground*. Pronunciation again enters the picture because careless pronunciation can cause misspelling. The consonant that is often left out is _____.

ground
background

54. The space behind closer areas is called back_____.
Thus in paintings the space farther back which provides
relief for the principal objects portrayed is the _____
_____.

background

55. A person's experience and training can also be called
_____.

REVIEW

a. *11*
b. *a*
c. *a*
d. *er*
e. *ti*
f. *a*
g. *ern*
h. *g*
i. *ron*
j. *e*

56. Fill in the missing letter(s).

a. fina____y   f. temper____ture

b. li__ble   g. gov_____ment

c. temper__ment   h. back__round

d. fed____al   i. envi_____ment

e. quan____ty   j. veg__table

a. environment
b. vegetable
c. liable
d. quantity
e. temperature
f. government
g. federal
h. finally
i. background
j. temperament

57. Complete the words matching these definitions.

a. surroundings   en_____

b. edible plant   veg_____

c. responsible   li_____

d. number   qu_____

e. heat or cold   tem_____

f. process of   gov_____
   ruling

g. referring to   fed_____
   central ruling

h. lastly   fi_____

i. space behind   back_____

j. manner of behaving tem_____

t

58. Mispronunciation also causes misspelling of the last
set of words. Take the noun *gratitude*. Pronouncing the
word carefully will produce a correctly spelled word:
grat i tude, not grad i tude. Which consonant in
the first syllable causes the difficulty? ____

grat i tude

59. Complete the first two syllables: _____ _____
tude.

gratitude

60. The noun which means thankfulness is _____.

gratitude

61. For all their kindness and generosity I expressed my deep _____.

a

62. Now pronounce *hundred* by syllables: hun dred. Which combination is at the beginning of the second syllable: (a) two consonants, or (b) a consonant and a vowel? _____

dr

63. Here you have the problem: *hun dred,* not hun derd. What consonants must precede the *e?* _____

hundred

64. The figure 100 stands for the word _____.

hundred

65. There were about a _____ people at the meeting.

second

66. The word *aggravate* is similar to *hundred* in that two consonants must precede the vowel to prevent the mis-spelling of the word. Pronounce it carefully: ag gra vate. Which syllable will cause the problem? _____

gr

67. In the second syllable what two consonants precede the vowel *a?* _____

aggravate

68. To make worse or make more of a trouble is the meaning of ag_____.

aggravate

69. In informal writing, to annoy or to vex can also be the meaning of _____.

og

70. If not correctly pronounced, the second syllable of *recognize* can cause trouble Through carelessness it is easy to omit which letters? rec___nize

rec og nize

71. Write the three syllables of this word: _____ _____ _____.

recognize

72. If we acknowledge people on the street we rec _____ them.

recognize

73. Only after careful study will I _____ the validity of your argument.

a. 3
b. *trag prej*
c. vowel
d. trag e dy
 prej u dice

74. The last two words take careful pronunciation and distinction of syllables: *tragedy* and *prejudice.* Pronounce them slowly, then answer these questions:

a. How many syllables does each have? _____

b. Each has only four letters in the first syllable: _____ and _____.

c. Each has a single (vowel, consonant) in the second syllable. _____

d. Now syllabify each word:

_____ _____ _____ and _____ _____ _____.

tragedy

75. A dramatic, disastrous event is called a tr_____.

tragedy

76. The terrible earthquake in Peru is a great _____.

prejudice

77. An adverse opinion or judgment made without sufficient knowledge is known as prej_____.

prejudice

78. Mr. Doe has allowed his life to be ruled by _____
_____.

REVIEW

a. aggravate
b. hundred
c. recognize
d. prejudice
e. gratitude
f. tragedy

79. Supply the correct words for these definitions.

a. To make worse is the meaning of _____.

b. The figure 100 is written like this: _____.

c. If you acknowledge a friend's fault, you _____ it.

d. Adverse judgment is called _____.

e. Thankfulness is the meaning of _____.

f. A dramatic, disastrous event is a _____.

POSTTEST

Every word you have studied in this chapter is included in the following sentences. Read each sentence carefully and from the context and meaning clue supply the missing words.

1. Last July the _____ soared into the 100s.

2. Ruth is a fine _____.
competitor in sports

3. It is a gr_____ matter.

4. Can you apply for a position with the _____ government?
central

5. I would like the necklace as a _____.
reminder

6. Tad will not eat a _____ with his meal.

7. People are affected by both heredity and _____.
surroundings

8. Black smoke poured from the _____.
smokestack

9. Do you have a sufficient _____ of tax forms?
amount

10. When will you be _____
                                    responsible
for paying your own debts?

11. Lucy has a nervous _____.

12. There were about a _____
                                    100
people present.

13. The new laws will only _____
                                    make worse
the situation.

14 Far too much _____
                                    bias
exists today.

15. Did he _____
                                    acknowledge
you when he passed you?

16. The transformer was struck by
_____.

17. The earthquake was _____.
                                    calamitous

18. The neighbor's child is very _____
_____.
                    playful

19. The teenager next door takes part
in _____.
                    sports

20. The sky is gradually _____
                                    becoming lighter
_____.

21. Their going will be a _____.

22. To play the hero's role well, Don
needs a good dramatic back_____.

23. Shakespeare's *Hamlet* is considered a great _____.

24. He ended his speech _____.
                                    at last

25. The newly formed nation has what
kind of _____?
                    political process

26. The young boy expressed his
_____.
            thankfulness

Chapter 2

PREFIXES

Confusing one prefix with another is easy to do, but learning not to is just as easy. How? By becoming aware of the part that pronunciation and meaning play in adding prefixes to the beginning of words, you can overcome this confusion quickly and surely. Misspelling certain words containing the Latin prefix *ad* is also easy to do, but by learning about assimilation you can easily eliminate such misspellings.

The objectives of this chapter are four: you will pronounce carefully words that include prefixes, such as *per-pre-pro* and *dis-de;* you will write the correct meaning for these and other troublesome prefixes; you will choose the correct prefix for particular root words; and you will write correctly a number of commonly misspelled words. Upon attaining these objectives, you will be better equipped to select the correct prefix for other words, familiar and unfamiliar, and spell accurately a number of words in which assimilation occurs.

PRETEST

A. Choose the correct spelling for each definition.

1. to scatter — diseminate, disseminate _diss_____
2. to spell incorrectly — mispell, misspell _misspell_____
3. not required — unnecessary, unecessary _unnecessary_____
4. to declare positively — afirm, affirm _affirm_____
5. to recall — recollect, reccollect _recollect_____
6. hostile action — agression, aggression _aggression_____

7. to differ   dissent, disent _dissent_

8. to make familiar   aquaint, acquaint _aquaint_

9. an error   misstake, mistake _mistake_

10. to cut up   disect, dissect _disect_

11. artificial   unnatural, unatural _unnatural_

12. to advise   reccommend, recommend _recommend_

13. to get   acquire, aquire _aquire_

B. Choose the correct prefix for each root word. Meanings are given to help you identify the words.

14. _per_ form   to act
    pre, (per)

15. _____pare   to get ready
    per, (pre) pro

16. _____service   an ill turn
    (dis,) de

17. _____ceed   to go ahead
    pre, (pro,) per

18. _____cede   to go before
    per, pro, (pre)

19. _____cide   come to a conclusion
    dis, (de)

20. _____scribe   denounce or condemn
    pre, per, (pro)

21. _____scribe   tell about something
    (dis,) de

22. _____scribe   set down as a rule
    (pre,) pro, per

a. dis
b. de
c. de
d. dis
e. de
f. dis
g. de

1. In certain words the prefixes _dis_ and _de_ have so similar a pronunciation that it is easy to substitute one for the other. The sound of _i_ in _dismiss_ and e in _describe_ is the same: the short sound of _i_. Because the sound is identical, the s following the e in describe provides the confusion: "dis cribe." The solution lies in the meaning of the prefix. _Dis_ means apart. If one is dismissed, one is sent apart. The prefix also means not. To dislike someone is not to like him or her. The prefix de has two meanings. First, it means down. If you descend, you go down. Second, it means off (or away). To deduct a dollar is to take it off (or away).

Consider the meanings of _dis_ and _de_ and choose the correct prefix for each root or base below. For bases not easily identified the meanings are given.

a. _dis_ approve   e. _de_ tour   (turn)

b. _de_ tain (hold)   f. _dis_ tend (stretch)

c. _de_ part (go)   g. _de_ cay (fall)

d. _dis_ trust

a. apart
b. off
c. down
d. not

2. Now write the correct meaning for each underlined prefix.

a. If you *dissect* a frog, you cut it _*A*_ .

b. If you *decide*, you cut _*B*_ deliberation.

c. If you *degrade* something, you grade it _*C*_ .

d. If you *distrust* people, you do _*d*_ have confidence in them.

a. not apart
b. down off (away)

3. Supply two meanings for each prefix.

a. *dis* _*Closed*_

b. *de* _*part*_

a. *dis*
b. *de*
c. *dis*
d. *de*
e. *dis*
f. *de*

4. Read these sentences carefully for their meaning, then supply the missing prefix, *dis* or *de*.

a. Their actions _*dis*_ honored the family name.

b. The mountaineers had difficulty trying to _*de*_ scend.

c. The supervisor's easygoing manner _*C*_ pelled the clerk's fears.

d. You should rewrite your _*dis*_ scription.

e. There is always a place in society for constructive _*de*_ sent.

f. After a while Sue became _*dis*_ spondent.

a. through
b. forward or forth
c. before

5. Confusing the prefixes *pre*, *per*, and *pro* usually results from similarities in pronunciation, from not knowing their meanings, and from not looking at them carefully. Since *you* can look at and pronounce these elements correctly, we are concerned here with their meanings:

pre   before
pro   forward or forth
per   through

For the following sentences write the correct meaning of each prefix.

a. A performer is one who carries an act _*through*_ .

b. A proposal is a plan that is brought _*forth*_ .

c. To precede is to go _*before*_ .

a. *per*
b. *pre*
c. *pro*
d. *per*

6. Now supply the correct missing prefix.

a. If you act or carry through you will _*per*_ form.

b. If you go before me you will _*pre*_ cede me.

c. To place an idea forward is to *pro*pose it.

d. To see all the way through is to *per*ceive it.

pre before
pro forward (forth)
per through

7. Write these three prefixes and their meanings.

pre means *before*

per means *through*

pro means *forth*

a. *per* through
b. *pre* before

c. *pro* forth
d. *per* through
e. *pro* forward
f. *pre* before

8. Read each sentence, then supply the correct prefix (*per-pre-pro*) and its meaning for each of these definitions.

a. To *per*meate is to soak _____.

b. To *pro*cede is to go *forth*.

c. To *pro*claim is to cry *forward*.

d. To _____forate is to punch holes _____ something.

e. A *pro*cession is a movement of people going *through*.

f. To *pre*cancel is to cancel a postage stamp *before* mailing.

REVIEW

a. *pre*
b. *per*
c. *de*
d. *de*
e. *de*
f. *de*
g. *dis*
h. *per* *per* *pro*
i. *pro*
j. *pro*
k. through
l. forward
m. before

9. Test your skill in choosing the correct prefixes or their meanings.

a. When my cousin had a severe reaction to the new drug, the doctor *per*scribed another drug.
per, pre

b. To sweat or excrete a fluid through the pores of the skin is to *per*spire.
pre, per

c. How many times must I *de*scribe her dress?
dis, de

d. A severe earthquake will *de*stroy even the well-constructed buildings.
dis, de

e. The father of the little boy is filled with grief and *de*spair.
de, dis

f. Senator Fowler stated that he could easily *de*spise all dishonest merchants.
dis, de

g. The constant drumming of his fingertips on the table will surely *dis*turb the patients.
de, dis

h. Instructors _per_ form duties _per_ taining to their
            pre, per   per, pre

pro fessions.
per, pre, pro

i. Even though I missed a month of school, the teachers decided to _pro_ mote me.
                    pre, pro

j. The high schools need a different _pro_ cedure for registration.
                 pro, pre

k. Perform means to act _through_ .
           through, before

l. To propose is to place _forward_ .
          before, forward

m. To precede is to go _before_ .
        through, before

a. apart not
b. down off (away)

10. Supply the meanings for these prefixes:

a. _dis_ _not_ or _APART_

b. _de_ _down_ or _off_

again back

11. The prefix _re_ can mean again or back. For instance, to reenter is to enter _again_ ; to recall some information is to call it _again_.

back again

12. Two commonly misspelled words are _recommend_ and _recollect_. Each contains the prefix _re_ and a root word. If we recollect, we recall or collect _again_ ; if we recommend we commend _back_ .

collect commend

13. These two words have the prefix _re_ and a root word. What are the roots? _recollect_ and _recommend_

recommend
recollect

14. If employees do good work, they are often _promoted_ _recommended_ ed for promotion.
  I find it hard to _recollect_ the exact details of the accident.

a. again
b. back
c. back
d. again

15. Now supply the correct meaning of _re_ in each word below.

a. request: to seek _again_

b. recall: to call _back_

c. a reprieve: a taking _back_

d. a reprint: a printing _again_

a. misstep
b. disservice
c. unnumbered
d. mistake
e. misstate
f. unnerved
g. mistreat
h. uncertainty
i. disrepair
j. dissolve

16. Most of the spelling problems with the prefixes *mis*, *dis*, and *un* come from forgetting that the prefix and the root are two entities. For example, *mis* ends in *s* and *spell* begins with *s*. When you combine them, you must keep both *s*'s. The same is true when you add *un* to a word beginning with *n*. With this in mind, add the specified prefixes and the roots below.

a. mis   step   *misstep*

b. dis   service   *disservice*

c. un   numbered   *unnumbered*

d. mis   take   *mistake*

e. mis   state   *mistate*

f. un   nerved   *unnerved*

g. mis   treat   *mistreat*

h. un   certainty   *uncertainly*

i. dis   repair   *disrepair*

j. dis   solve   *dissolve*

a. c.

17. Some words are derived from a Latin root and the prefix *ad*, meaning to, toward, or near to, or used as an intensive. Take *adhere:* it comes from *ad* (toward) and *haērer* (stick). If you apply glue to a piece of paper it "sticks toward" or adheres. Another word is *acclaim: ad* (to) *clāmāre* (shout), to applaud. Note that the *d* from *ad* is absent.

If you pronounce *adhere* rapidly several times, the sound of the *d* does *not* change. If you pronounce *ad claim* in the same manner, the sound *does* change; it becomes muted and similar to the adjacent sound ("k" sound in claim). In other words, assimilation has taken place. To account for the *d*, the same sound ("k") is substituted—in this case the same letter: *ac claim.*

Pronounce the following combinations rapidly several times. In which ones is the *d not* assimilated? _____

a. ad   minister   c. ad   mire
b. ad   firm   d. ad   gression

a.
b.
d.
f.

18. Look at these words and their origins, then pronounce them rapidly. In which ones *is* the *d* assimilated? _____

a. ad ply (*ad plicāre*) to fold together

b. ad gregate (*ad gregāre*) to herd
c. ad monish (*ad monēre*) to remind
d. ad semble (*ad simul*) together
e. ad mit (*ad mittere*) to send in to
f. ad lure (*ad leurrer*) to lure

affirm

19. In assimilation the sound of the *d* in *ad* becomes similar to the sound of the beginning letter of the root. What is the correct spelling of *ad firm*? _____

a. apply
b. aggregate
c. assemble
d. allure

20. And the correct spelling of

a. ad ply _____

b. ad gregate _____

c. ad semble _____

d. ad lure _____

accurately

21. A common English word has this origin: *ad cūrāre*, to care for. If one "cares for" a job, one tries to do it _____curately.

assist

22. Another common word has this origin: *ad sistere*, to stand near. If I stand near you, or help you, I _____sist you.

aggravation

23. In the combination *ad* and *gravāre*, the root means to burden and *ad* is an intensive (the burden is indeed heavy). Such a burden is an _____gravation.

the root has an
a (gra̱vare)

24. How does the word origin signal that *aggrevation* is a misspelling? _____

_____

a. appear
b. aggression
c. applaud
d. attest

25. Decide if the *d* is assimilated, then complete the spelling of the modern English words.

a. *ad pārēre* (to show) _____pear

b. *ad gradī* (step toward) _____gression

c. *ad plaudere* (to clap) _____plaud

d. *ad testārī* (to be witness) _____test

hard *c*

26. Assimilation also occurs in words like *acquire* and *acquaint*. Their derivations are *ad* (to) *quaerere* (seek, obtain) and *ad* (intensive) *cognōscere* (to know). In these words we do not find the first letter of the root doubled, but we do find the sound doubled. In other words, the

"k" sound of *quaint* and *quire* is the same as the _____
hard, soft
sound of _____ in the prefix.

acquire
acquainted

27. If we "obtain" we _____quire. If we "know" we be-come _____quainted with something.

acquire
acquainted

28. When will Dan Williams _____ the chemical plant? I didn't know you were _____ with the governor.

REVIEW

a. recommend
b. recollect (or recall)
c. appalled
d. recommendation
e. ally
f. unnatural
g. misspelled
h. substitute p for d
i. unnecessary
j. first g, first a
k. to show the presence of d
l. dissatisfied
m. acquire
n. misstated
o. acquaintance
p. mistakes

29. Read the sentences carefully, then write the required word or phrase.

a. To commend again is to _____.

b. To call back some information is to _____ it.

c. A modern English word is derived from the Latin *ad* and *palir* (to grow pale). If we see a situation and "grow pale," we are _____palled.

d. Because of Lou's poor work record I cannot write a _____ation.

e. *Ad* and *ligāre* means to bind to. The person who be-comes "bound to" another in a venture is an _____ly.

f. Their behavior is _____.
un natural

g. Why are so many words _____?
mis spelled

h. If you pronounce rapidly *ad* and *praise* (to evaluate), the *d* is assimilated. To indicate its presence in spelling, you _____.

i. Your explanation is _____.
un necessary

j. What are the critical spots in *aggravate?* _____

k. Why is c present in *acquire* and *acquaint?* _____

l. After using the new product for a month, I am _____
dis satisfied

m. To obtain is the meaning of _____quire.

n. He has _____ the facts.
mis stated

o. A person one knows slightly is an _acquaint_ance.

p. The clerk makes far too many _____ _Unistakes_
~~mis takes~~

in typing.

POSTTEST

Choose the correct prefix.

1. To sweat means to ___per___spire.
pro, per, pre

2. I asked the doctor for a new
_____scription.
(pro,) pre, de

3. Mr. Roe finally _____suaded the
pre, (per)
visitor to leave.

4. He felt nothing but absolute _____
(dis,) de
spair.

5. To set above in favor is the meaning of _____fer.
pro, (pre)

6. In ten minutes the black ink
_____meated the rug.
per, pro, pre

7. Can you _____scribe the sunset?
dis, de

8. Before I finished my rebuttal of
the first point, I was ordered to
_____ceed to the next.
pre, pro, per

9. I could not _____sect the frog.
de, dis

10. The doctor granted _____mission
pre, per
to go home.

Supply the prefix meaning for each sentence.

11. In destroying you are tearing
_____.

12. Permanent means changeless, or
remaining _____out.

13. A distraction is something that
draws you _____.

14. To recall is to call _____.

15. The state of being perplexed is
to be literally "entwined" all the
way _____.

16. To disserve is to treat badly, or
_____ to serve one.

17. If you desist, you abstain from
doing something, or you stand _____
_____.

18. When you precede another, you
go _____ that person.

19. A person's decease (or death) is
a going _____.

20. Someone who is disreputable
is _____ reputable.

Test your skill by answering these questions correctly.

21. What is the Latin prefix in *appear,
attest, accuse?* _____

24. A star's dynamic personality can
_____tract many fans.

22. Combine the Latin prefix *ad* and the root *point* (to point) into a modern English word. _____

23. Frieda is not a friend, only an _____ .

25. Combine the prefix *ad* and the root *quit* into a modern English word. _____

26. First aid was _____ministered to the stricken _____sembly.

Chapter 3

SYLLABICATION

Although etymology and pronunciation can be helpful in spelling words correctly, syllabication can be the answer for particularly troublesome words. To divide words into syllables you need to know about vowels, semivowels, dipthongs, consonants, long and short sounds of vowels, and major and minor stress. If you are not familiar with all this, or if you need a refresher, work through Appendix A before you begin this chapter. If you need only the guidelines begin with frame 13 of the appendix. Because the material in this chapter is predicated on your knowing how to syllabify words, it might be worth your while to work the entire appendix anyway. At any rate the pretest to the appendix can tell you immediately whether you should or should not.

In this chapter you will (1) learn a five-step method of spelling words through syllabication; (2) use this method in spelling specific words; (3) recognize what elements in words to look and listen for; (4) spell a number of words in and out of context; and (5) reproduce these words from definition clues. It is hoped that you will use this reliable method in spelling unfamiliar and other familiar but bothersome words.

PRETEST

Fill in the missing letters. Meanings are given to help you identify the words.

1. in_____est   concern, curiosity
2. embar_____   make ill at ease
3. irrel_e_vant   not related
4. ser_vice_   noncommissioned rank in Army
5. vil_la_n_   scoundrel

6. expe_____ knowledge, skill

7. ac_____ get possession of

8. im_____ately right now

9. dis_____faction displeasure

10. vac_____ cleaning appliance

11. ap_____ent readily seen or understood

12. con_____ience comfort

13. pro____dure method of proceeding

14. oc_____ally from time to time

15. disap_____ not come up to expectations

16. lon_____ness dejection and sadness

17. op_____nity occasion

18. fin____cier expert in finance

19. discrim____ation prejudice

20. par_____el going same direction

21. ac_____late amass, gather

22. disap_____ vanish

23. inter_____ break between

24. res_____ eating place

25. ap_____ciate recognize, become aware of

26. ac_____ance someone you know slightly

27. ex_____ation act of explaining

28. ac_____plishment act of succeeding

29. pos_____sion ownership

1. Several words have what is called the "double conso-nant" difficulty: sometimes an extra consonant is added, other times a consonant is omitted. We shall eliminate the problem by establishing a procedure for dividing words into syllables.

(1) Look at the word carefully (look for familiar roots, prefixes, suffixes, double letters, and the like).

(2) Say the word distinctly and correctly. If you are not sure about the pronunciation, check the dictionary. Look for pronounced vowels as a guide to the number of syllables.

a. both
yes
· · · · · · · · · · · · ·
b. 4
4
short
· · · · · · · · · · · · ·
c. ac com plish
   ment
d. accomplishment
· · · · · · · · · · · · ·
e. accomplishment

(3) Sound the word in syllables and then write it.

(4) Write the word from memory and check for the correct spelling.

(5) Use it in sentences. Be sure you know what the word means.

a. Now take the word *accomplishment*. Look at it carefully. Do you find a prefix or a suffix or (both)? _____
Do you find a double consonant? *yes*
· ·

b. Now pronounce it. How many pronounced vowels does it have? *4* How many syllables are there? *4* Does the second syllable have a short or long sound of o?
short
· ·

c. Mentally sound the word as you write it in syllables:
AC   Comp plish   ment.
d. Write it quickly from memory:
Accomplishment.
· ·

e. Use it in one or more sentences. The professor told me that my reaching the quota was quite an *Accomplishment*
_____.

look
say (pronounce)
in syllables
in sentences

2. To review the procedure: you first *look* at the word carefully, then *say* it distinctly, sound out and write the word (as a whole, in syllables) write it from memory and check the spelling, and finally use it (in phrases, (in sentences)) _____.

4
ac cu mu late

3. Here is the second word *accumulate*, which means to amass or gather. Perform the first two steps on your own. How many syllables are there? *4* What are they?
Ac Cum mu late

accumulate

4. Write the word from memory: *Accumulate*.

a. accumulate
b. accumulate

5. Now use it in context:

a. Jane's father exclaimed, "How many books did you *Accumulate* in a year!"

b. This house can *Accumulate* more dust than any other I've known.

ap pre ci ate

6. The next four words also have a double consonant difficulty. The first is *appreciate*. In mastering the spelling of this word, you first look at it carefully, pronounce it distinctly, and then divide it into syllables: _____
_____.

appreciate

7. The word which means to estimate the value of something or to fully realize a situation is _____.

appreciate
appreciate

8. Even though I haven't been poverty-stricken, I think I can _____ the dire problems involved.
   realize
   Professors _____ the efforts of
   value
their students.

3 *p*
• • • • • • • • • • • •
ap par ent
apparent

9. On your own perform the first two steps with the word *apparent*. It has ____ syllables and a double consonant ____ near the beginning of the word.
• •
Perform the third step: _____.
And now the fourth: _____.

apparent
apparent
apparent

10. To be readily understood is the definition of the word _____.
That he has a mastery of his subject is _____.
Are my feelings about religion that _____?

c
oc ca sion al ly

11. Look carefully at the adverb *occasionally*. It has only one s but it has two ____'s.
Now divide it into syllables: _____.

occasionally
occasionally
occasionally

12. Write it quickly from memory: _____.
Now use it in these sentences:
I go to the theater _____.
Will you accompany me _____ to the symphony concerts?

op por tu ni ty

13. Here is the word *opportunity*. Look at it . . . pronounce it . . . and remembering the guidelines for a long and short vowel, divide it into syllables: _____
_____.

a. opportunity
b. opportunity

14. Combine the fourth and fifth steps:

a. The noun that means a suitable occasion or time is _____.

b. Will we ever have an _____ to meet the famous pitcher?

occasiona*lly*

15. Fill in the missing letters: oc␣asional_ly_.

a. accumulate
b. occasionally
c. appreciate
d. accomplishment
e. opportunity
f. apparent

REVIEW

16. From the meaning clues supply the appropriate words you have just studied.

a. The verb meaning to amass is _____.

b. We used to drive to the ranch every Sunday; now we go only _____.

c. No matter what the outcome is, I do _____

value
your efforts to promote the campaign.

d. After reviewing Jim's work in art history, the instructor said, "That's quite an _____!"

successful completion

e. I've never had the _____ to attend

occasion
a drama festival.

f. She made her intentions quite _____.

readily understood

first
4
dis sat is fac tion

17. Here are four words with the same beginning, the prefix *dis*. Remember that a prefix is a separate unit, so the addition of a prefix usually does not disturb the word or the prefix. The noun *dissatisfaction* is simply the combination of *satisfaction* and *dis* (meaning not), so the whole word means a state of not being satisfied, or displeasure. Look at the word carefully and then pronounce it.
Which syllable is the prefix? _____
How many other syllables are there? _____
Write the word in syllables: _____.

a. dissatisfaction
b. dissatisfaction

18. Use the word in these contexts:

a. To have a feeling of displeasure is to have one of _____.

b. Mr. Brown registered his _____ by shouting at the delegate.

dissatisfaction

19. The new wage proposals caused the most _____ _____ among the lowest paid drivers.

prefix
crim i na tion

20. Perform the first two steps for this word: *discrimination*. *Dis* is a (prefix, suffix) _____. Now divide the rest of the word into syllables, watching your vowel sounds: _____.

discrimination

21. This word has two common meanings. The first is an act of prejudice: There is too much _____ between the races and sexes.

discrimination

22. Another meaning is the ability to see fine distinctions: In his reviews of operatic performances, Mr. Bucher shows a keen _____.

dis p

23. *Disappoint* and *disappear* have two similarities: both have the prefix _____ and both have a double _____ in the root.

dis ap point
dis ap pear

24. Now pronounce the words and separate each into syllables: _____

a. disappear
b. disappoint
c. disappoint
d. disappear

25. Read the sentences and write the correct one of these two words for each.

a. Perhaps I can catch them before they _____ from sight.

b. If you don't go with me, you will _____ me.

c. When students do not work hard, they often _____ _____ their teachers.

d. In time the trumpeter swan may _____.

im me di ate ly

26. The next group of words also has double consonant difficulties. The first is *immediately*. Perform the first two steps . . . now divide it into syllables: _____

immediately

27. To respond without hesitation or delay is to answer _____.

immediately

28. The children were trained to reply _____.

3
s

29. The second word in this group is *possession*. Look . . . pronounce . . . how many syllables does the word have? ___ There are two sets of ___'s.

pos ses sion

30. Now divide it:_____.

possessions

31. A few clothes and a toothbrush comprise his worldly _____.

possession

32. There is an old saying that _____
                                    ownership
is nine-tenths of the law.

yes

I

par al lel

33. Perform the initial steps for this word: *parallel*.
Does it have a double letter? _____
What is it? _____
What are the syllables? _____

second   third

34. One of the double letters completes the _____
syllable and the second begins the _____ syllable.

II

35. The two *l*'s standing so nicely together match the
geometric definition of the word: two (or more) straight
lines that do not intersect. Look for the straight lines in
para_____el.

parallel

36. This word also means having comparable parts: The
construction of the two sentences is _____.

em bar rass

37. The word *embarrass* can best be spelled correctly by
dividing it into syllables. But first look at it . . . then pronounce it . . . and now divide it: _____.

embarrass

38. To cause someone to be ill at ease or to hamper with
financial difficulties are definitions of the word _____
_____.

embarrass

39. Jack's intention was to _____ the assembly.

REVIEW

a. dissatisfaction
b. disappear
c. parallel
d. possession
e. discrimination
f. immediately
g. embarrass
h. disappoint

40. From the clues presented in each sentence, write the
correct word for each.

a. Reverend Dunn showed his _____
displeasure
with the program by closing the hall.

b. The minute I suggest their doing the dishes, they
_____.
vanish

c. Your red dots are not _____.
comparable

d. How many appliances do you have in your pos_____
_____?

e. Now there are laws against _____.
prejudice

f. May I return the book tomorrow or do you want it
_____?
right now

g. I was afraid to tell her because I might _____

put ill at ease

her.

h. I surely hope Mrs. Brown doesn't _____

fail to meet expectations

me.

first
1 2
ac quire
ac quain tance

41. Two words often misspelled have the same begin-ning: *acquire* and *acquaintance.* The misspelling is caused partly by poor pronunciation and partly by not studying the word. Perform the first two steps on your own.
Since *ac* is the prefix it is the _____ syllable in each word.
How many syllables are left in acquire? _____ in acquaint-ance? _____
Now syllabify the two words: _____ and
_____.

acquire

42. If Mr. Hancock wants to get possession of 10 percent of his company's stock, he wants to _____ it.

acquaintance

43. A person you know less intimately than a friend is called an _____.

a. acquire
b. acquaintance
c. acquaintances
d. acquire

44. Write the correct word of these two in the following sentences.

a. Randy wants to _____ two lakeshore lots.

b. Jack is not a friend; he is only an _____.

c. Most people have quite a few _____.

d. Tom has worked hard to _____ all his trophies.

prefix (or *ir*)
3
(ir) rel e vant

45. Perform the first two steps for *irrelevant* (*ir* is a variant of the prefix *in,* meaning not).
What constitutes the first syllable? _____
How many more syllables are there? _____
What are they? _____

irrelevant

46. Write the word from memory: _____.

irrelevant

47. That which has no bearing on a particular case is
_____.

irrelevant

48. The teacher commented that some of my evidence was _____.

2
1
r
in ter rupt

49. The word *interrupt* is derived from the Latin *inter*, meaning between, and *rumpere*, to break. Look at and pronounce the word carefully.
How many syllables does the prefix have? _____
How many remaining syllables are there? _____
What letter ends the prefix and also begins the root? _____
Write the syllables: _____.

interrupt

50. The word meaning to stop or break the continuity of is _____.

interrupt

51. If you "break between" two persons carrying on a conversation, you will _____ them.

interrupt irrelevant

52. The chairperson threatened to _____ the delegate's speech if some of the points were_____.
                                                                    not related

3
3
e in first syllable
yes—suffix (ness)

53. The word *loneliness* presents no real problem as long as you look at it and pronounce it carefully.
How many pronounced vowels does it have? _____
How many syllables are there? _____
What vowel is not pronounced? _____
Are there added elements (prefix or suffix)? _____

lone li ness

54. Now for the syllables: _____.

loneliness

55. If one is dejected, perhaps a bit sad, he is lonely; the state of being dejected is called _____.

loneliness

56. Although surrounded by many friends, Sam lives a life of _____.

ex pla na tion
pro ce dure

57. The spelling of these next words depends on your pronunciation of them and on your looking at them closely. Take *explanation* first and perform the first two steps. Then do the same for *procedure*. If you have done your work carefully, you can now divide them easily: _____
_____   _____.

explanation
procedure

58. Write both words from memory: _____
_____.

ex *pla* nation
pro ce dure

59. Notice that the last syllable of the verb *explain* is not spelled like the second syllable of the related noun: ex____nation. Neither is the last syllable of *proceed* spelled like the second syllable of its related noun: pro____dure.

explanation
procedure

a. explanation
b. procedure
c. explanation
   procedure

60. To explain a point is to offer an _____ ;
a manner of proceeding is called a _____ .

61. Choose one or the other of these two words to fit the
sentences below.

a. I doubt if he can give me a good _____ .

b. I wonder what _____ he will initiate.

c. The noun that relates to explain is _____ ;
the one that relates to proceed is _____ .

REVIEW

a. irrelevant
b. acquaintance
c. loneliness
d. procedure
e. acquire
f. explanation
g. procedure

62. From the contexts, write the appropriate words.

a. If a point is not related, it is _Irrelevant_ .

b. Someone you know slightly can be called an _Acqu
Aintance_ .

c. The doctor cannot rouse him from his state of _____
loneliness .
        dejection

d. What will be the _Procedure_ at the convention?
                    method

e. How long will it take to ~~possess~~ _acquire_ the property?
                    possess

f. He gave a lengthy _____ of the new
law.

g. Are you sure this is the right _____ ?
                    manner of proceeding

4
ex
ence

63. The word *experience* can present a problem, but only
momentarily. First look at it, then pronounce it.
How many syllables has it? _____
What is the prefix? _____
What is the suffix? _____

e

64. We have the first and last syllables—now to divide
to make the second and third: ex   peri   ence. Pronounce
it again. Although the first vowel does not have a long
sound as the r colors it, it is closer to this sound than
to the short sound of e. Therefore, to get the second
syllable you would divide after which letter? _____

ex pe ri ence

65. Now divide the whole word: _____ .

experience

66. An event lived through is the definition of the word
_____.

experience

67. A person can also _____ a feeling of loneliness.

3
con
ience
ven

68. Although the last part of the word _convenience_ is similar to _experience_, it is not pronounced the same. The last syllable (_ience_) has the sound of "yens." With this difference in mind, perform steps (1) and (2).
How many syllables are there? _____
The first syllable is the prefix _____.
The last syllable is _____.
The middle syllable is _____.

con ven ience

69. Now write the three syllables: _____.

convenience

70. A personal comfort, or something that increases comfort, like a toaster or fry pan, is a _____.

convenience

71. Because many packaged foods are easy to prepare, they're often called _____ items.

2
first _l_
vil lain

72. Look at and pronounce this word: _villain._
How many syllables are there? _____
Where do you divide after the first? _____
Divide the word into syllables: _____.

villain

73. A scoundrel can be called a _____.

villain

74. In a melodrama the character usually hissed at and booed by the audience is the _____.

3

75. _Interest_ can be pronounced correctly with two or three syllables. But the spelling always has how many syllables? _____

interest

76. To hold the attention of a person is to in_____ him.

interest

77. A feeling of curiosity or fascination is the definition of the noun _____.

vac u um

78. Like _interest_, the word _vacuum_ can be pronounced in two or three syllables, but to spell it correctly you must divide it graphically into three parts. Apply your guidelines and divide this word: _____.

vacuum vacuum

79. A space empty of matter is called a vac_____. A feeling of emptiness can be known as a _____.

vacuum

80. The electric appliance to clean rugs is also called a

_____.

res
tau   rant

81. Two words, derived from Old French, have retained the spelling characteristics of the French language. The first is *restaurant.* If you remember the guideline about two consonants between two vowels, you can form the first syllable easily. What is the first syllable? _____.
The rest of the word falls naturally into two syllables:

_____   _____.

restaurant

82. An eating place is called a _____.

fin
an   cier

83. The second word that has retained the French spelling is *financier,* an expert in financial affairs. The short vowel at the beginning gives the clue to the first syllable:

_____.
The rest of the word is easy to divide: _____.

financier

84. An expert in large-scale money affairs is known as a

_____.

financier

85. J. P. Morgan was a famous American _____.

3
is not
2
vowel is the same—
sergeant, servire

86. *Sergeant* also has a French "flavor" as its derivation goes back to Old French; however, its basic origin is the Latin verb *servire,* to serve. Pronunciation alone will not give you the necessary clues to correct spelling, so observe it closely.
How many vowels does it have? _____
The *a* in the second syllable (is, is not) pronounced?
So there are how many syllables? _____
What is the relationship of the first vowel in *sergeant* to the original Latin verb? _____

ser   geant

87. Now divide the word: _____.

sergeant

88. One of the noncommissioned officer ranks in the Army is that of _____.

REVIEW

a. experience
b. villain
c. interest
d. convenience
e. sergeant
f. restaurant

89. From the clues given below write the correct word for each sentence.

a. John could not get the teaching position because he lacked ex_____.

b. The role I like to portray best is the _____.

g. financier
h. vacuum

c. I don't have any in_____ in collecting stamps.

d. Living a block from the store is a _____.
   comfort

e. Lance was promoted to s_____.

f. Dining at a _____ is expensive.

g. An expert in financial affairs is a _____.

h. My niece bought a new _____.
   rug cleaner

POSTTEST

Write the complete word. The beginning of each word and the meaning are given to help you identify them.

1. vac_____ cleaning appliance

2. vil_____ scoundrel

3. in_____ concern

4. s_____ noncommissioned officer rank

5. em_____ make ill at ease

6. ac_____ get possession of

7. dis_____ vanish

8. ex_____ knowledge, skill

9. im*mediately* this minute

10. pro_____ method of proceeding

11. oc_____ now and then

12. lo_____ state of dejection

13. fin_____ financial expert

14. ap_____ readily seen

15. dis_____ prejudice

16. ac_____ amass, gather

17. op_____ occasion

18. con_____ comfort

19. inter_____ break between

20. ac_____ person slightly known

21. dis_____ displeasure

22. res_____ eating place

23. ap_____ be aware of
24. dis_____ fail to come up to expectation
25. ex_____ act of explaining
26. ac_____ment act of succeeding
27. par_____ same direction, similar
28. pos_____ ownership
29. ir_____ not related

Chapter 4

SILENT LETTERS

If you have had words marked off because you left out a letter that was not sounded, usually called a silent letter, you may have wondered why the letter was there in the first place. In the Middle English period (the twelfth through the fifteenth centuries), some of the final e's and all the consonants were pronounced. For example, the *k* and *gh* in *knight* and the *k* in *know* were sounded. Many words from the Greek had initial letters sounded, like the *p* in *psychology* and *pneumonia*. Gradually the pronunciation of many words changed, some letters becoming silent. The fact that they are still silent does not mean that they are to be omitted. On the contrary, they are there to stay until such time as the spelling is changed. In this chapter, then, you will (1) recognize the relationship between the derivation and the present word; (2) practice spelling a number of useful words in and out of context; and (3) reproduce the words from given definitions. Remember that the meaning and the spelling of words are both important.

PRETEST

Fill in the missing letters. The definitions given will help you to identify the words.

1. W_____nesday   a day of the week
2. d_eb_t   something owed
3. con_____   criticize severely
4. g_____ian   one who protects
5. _____ology   study of the mind
6. r____thm   recurring motion, measure
7. _____ledge   learning

8. und_____edly   beyond hesitation

9. ex_____st   to tire or wear out

10. g_____   to protect

11. s____tle   clever

12. ___riter   one who composes

13. _____iatry   medical treatment of the mind

14. dou__t   hesitate or waver

---

debt
doubt
undoubtedly
subtle

1. Four useful words have the same silent letter, having been derived from these Latin words: *debere*, meaning to owe; *dubitare*, meaning to waver; and *subtilis*, meaning thin and fine.
If you owe something you have a de__t.
If you hesitate or waver, you dou__t; if there is no wavering, you will undou__tedly succeed.
If you can make fine distinctions, or are clever, you are su__tle.

a. debt
b. doubt
c. undoubtedly
d. subtle

2. According to the context, write or complete these same four words.

a. When you haven't paid a bill, you still have a _____.

b. If you are in _____, do nothing.

c. The word that means accepted without doubt is un_____.

d. If one can make a point so "fine" as to be elusive or abstruse, he is said to be _____tle.

a. subtle
b. doubt
c. undoubtedly
d. debts

3. Now fit these four words into these contexts.

a. She has a reputation for being _____.

b. Why must they _____ everything I say?

c. He is _____ the most stubborn person I know.

d. Alex filed for bankruptcy because he had so many _____.

d

4. The word *Wednesday* comes from the Old English *Wodnesdaeg*, or "Woden's Day." Woden, as you may remember, was the chief Teutonic god, and because Wednesday relates directly to this proper name, it is right that the first syllable end in _____.

Woden's	**5.** You can best remember the silent letter in this word by recalling _____ Day.
Wednesday	**6.** The day after Tuesday is _____nesday.
Wednesday	**7.** Sometimes Valentine's Day comes on _____.
h	**8.** Now pronounce the words *exhaust* and *rhythm* carefully. Which letter is not sounded? _____
does	**9.** The words are derived from the Latin *exhaurire* and *rhythmus*. Examine these words carefully. The origin of the English words (does, does not) account for the silent letter. _____
h	**10.** *Exhaurire* means to draw out, so if a long car ride draws the passengers out, it ex___austs them.
exhaust	**11.** To tire out is to ex_____.
exhaust	**12.** The legislator will soon _____ the listeners.
rhythm	**13.** The Latin word *rhythmus* means recurring motion or measure, so the English word meaning a regular beat in music is _____thm.
rhythm	**14.** The three basics of music are melody, harmony, and _____.
rhythm	**15.** Some modern artists have an altogether new sense of _____.
rhythm exhaust	**16.** The monotonous _____ of the windshield wiper will eventually annoy and _____ the elderly driver.
knowledge	**17.** If *know* means to learn and understand, the understanding gained through experience and study is _____ledge.
first	**18.** The silent letter in the word that means understanding or learning is at the beginning of which syllable? _____
knowledge	**19.** He surprises me with his _____.
knowledge	**20.** Despite all his _____, he is quite illogical at times.

REVIEW

a. Wednesday
b. doubt
c. debts
d. rhythm
e. undoubtedly
f. exhaust
g. knowledge
h. subtle

21. Write the silent letter words for these sentences.

a. What day precedes Thursday? _____

b. How long will you _____ his motives?
                                       hesitate over

c. You owe far too many _____.

d. The three essentials of music are melody, harmony, and _____.

e. He is _____ the finest jazz trombonist
                without hesitation
today.

f. I am afraid that a long journey will _____
                                    tire out
my grandfather.

g. Sometimes a little _____ is a handicap.
                                learning

h. The distinction between the two is quite _____.

n

22. When you pronounce the verb *condemn*, which letter is not sounded? _____

yes

23. The word comes from the Latin *condemnare*. Is the silent letter related to the original word? _____

condemns

24. The Latin word means to damage, so if one "damages" another, one expresses severe disapproval—in other words, one con_____ that person.

condemn

25. To censure or criticize severely is to _____.

condemned

26. Even before the trial, he was called a _____ed man.

end

27. Unlike the word *knowledge*, *condemn* has the silent letter at the _____ of the word.

p

28. Three words, *psychology*, *psychiatry*, and *psychopathy* are derived from the Greek word *psukhe*. Each word has the silent letter _____.

psychology

29. *Psukhe* means life, breath, soul, and *ology* is an ending meaning study. From these two is produced the word meaning the study of the mind or mental processes _____.

psychiatry

30. Since the ending *iatry* indicates medical treatment, the treatment of the mind is called _____.

psychopathy

31. The ending *pathy* indicates disease. Disease of the mind, or mental disorder, can be called _____ *opathy.*

psychology
psychiatry
psychopathy

32. The study of mental processes is _____; the medical treatment of the mind is _____; and a form of mental disease is _____.

u

33. The words *guard* and *guardian* have a common derivation: from Old French *garder* or *guarder*, from the Germanic. Here you find a shift in the spelling of the French verb, but the English words have retained the silent _____.

guard   guardian

34. To watch over is the meaning of the word _____; and the one who watches over is called a _____ian.

guard

35. To take precautions is also the meaning of the root word: the hospital tries to _____ against infection.

guardhouse
guardroom

36. The detention house for military personnel is called a _____house; the room in which prisoners are confined is a _____room.

writes

37. The last word to be studied is one of the most common in the English language and also one of the most often misspelled. It is derived from Old English *writan* meaning to tear or scratch. If one scratches out a message, one _____ it.

is w

38. The Old English word for tear or scratch indicates that the origin of the current word (is, is not) responsible for the inclusion of the silent letter _____.

write
writing   writer

39. The verb that means to form words and sentences is _____. The act of putting this down is _____ing, and the person who puts it down is the _____er.

w t

40. All three words have the silent ____ and only one ____ after the *i.*

writers
writing

41. Both my father and brother are famous _____; in fact, they are _____ novels at present.

REVIEW

a. condemn
b. psychology
c. guardian
d. writers
e. psychiatry
f. guard
g. writing
h. psychopathy

42. Complete or write the silent letter word for each sentence.

a. Some people like to con_____ before knowing the
                  criticize
facts.

b. My cousin is majoring in _____.
                     study of the mind

c. My aunt now needs a legal _____.
                  protector

d. We have several _____ in the family.
               authors

e. Medical treatment of the mind is called _____iatry.

f. To watch over is to _____.

g. The young boy is _____ a short story.
               composing

h. One form of mental disorder is _____opathy.

POSTTEST

From the meaning of each sentence, or the meaning clue, supply the correct silent letter word.

1. To protect is to _____.

2. A difficult art to master is the art of _____ing.

3. The study of the mental processes is _____.

4. To hesitate to believe people is to _____them.

5. The day after Tuesday is _____.

6. The rain fell in a steady _____.
               measure or beat

7. He tried to impress us with his _____.
        learning

8. The girl bought so many articles on time that she was always in _____.

9. To criticize severely is to _____.

10. A legal protector is usually called a _____.

11. A person clever enough to make extremely fine distinctions is said to be _____.

12. Beyond hesitation is the definition of _____.

13. To tire out is the meaning of _____.

14. One who writes is a _____.

15. The medical treatment of the problems of the mind is _____.

Chapter 5

VOWEL STRESS

Perhaps one of the biggest problems in spelling is trying to identify vowel sounds when they are not distinct. At times correct pronunciation does help because we do mispronounce or slur vowels. Most of the time, however, vowel sounds that cause trouble cannot be classified as long or short sounds, or even approaching one or the other. For example, because the first *i* in *definite* receives little stress, making it unrecognizable as any kind of "i" sound, the word is often misspelled. Such unstressed sounds (or reduced vowels as they are sometimes called) appear in many words, so it is important for you to recognize this problem.

In this chapter, then, you will (1) become aware of the difficulties that unstressed (or lightly stressed) vowels present; (2) recognize these sounds and the syllables in which they appear; (3) spell a number of useful words with such vowel sounds, both in and out of context; and (4) from various contexts or definitions, reproduce the specific words in the chapter. In addition, it is hoped that you will become doubly conscious of unstressed and lightly stressed vowels and apply what you learn here to the spelling of other words.

PRETEST

Fill in the missing letter(s).

1. ben___fit
2. gramm___r
3. opt___mism
4. famil_____
5. hum___rous

6. compar___tive
7. r___diculous
8. elim___nate
9. sim___lar
10. dom___nant

11. warr___nt
12. cand___date
13. sent___nce
14. mand___tory
15. dorm___tory

16. math___matics

17. sacr___fice

18. contr___versy

19. ___pinion

20. crit___cism

21. sep___rate

22. def___nite

23. calend___r

24. legit___mate

25. cat___gory

26. d___vide

27. prob___bly

28. fasc___nate

29. partic___l___r

30. priv___lege

31. lab___ratory

32. pecul_____

33. bull___tin

34. intell___gence

---

does

1. The first syllable of *ridiculous* (ri) has a slightly stressed vowel. If you mispronounce or slur this word you may choose the wrong vowel to represent the sound. First pronounce the word: ri dic u lous. In the second syllable *dic* the *i* has a short *i* sound as in *pick.* The first *i* (does, does not) have the same sound.

short

2. If you said "does not" you undoubtedly slurred that first *i*. In spelling this word, always remember that the vowel in the first and second syllables has the (long, short) sound of *i*. _____

ridiculous

3. Silly or laughable is one definition of _____ulous.

ridiculous

4. Deserving or inspiring ridicule is also a definition of

_____.

short

5. Like *ridiculous*, the word *divide* has a first vowel sound that must be correctly spoken and heard. And like the first syllable in *ridiculous*, the first syllable in this word has the (long, short) sound of *i*. _____

divide

6. To separate into parts is the meaning of _____vide.

divide

7. If no agreement in policy is reached, the assembly will _____ into factions.

pin (second)
o (first)

8. Like the slightly stressed vowel, the vowel that receives the least amount of stress in a word or hardly any stress at all, causes a problem. Take *opinion*, for example. Pronounce it and indicate which syllable receives the most stress: o pin ion. _____. Which syllable receives the least stress? _____

o

9. Because the vowel is not easily recognized as an o you must, in spelling the word, stress the letter in some way. Like this: opinion—or perhaps connect it with the verb *opine*, meaning to think. *Opine* has a distinct sound of the vowel ___.

opinion

10. A conclusion one holds or an evaluation based on special knowledge are two definitions of _____.

tic (second)
little

11. Now take the word *particular*. It is syllabified like this: par tic u lar. Say the word quickly, noting how much stress each syllable receives. Which syllable receives the most? _____
Do the other syllables have (some or little) stress? _____

par (first) *lar* (last)

12. Unstressed vowels are not easy to distinguish, so pronunciation alone may not solve the problem. Emphasizing the vowel sounds and looking at the word carefully will help. Which syllables are similar: par tic u lar?
_____.

particular

13. Now write the word from memory: _____.

particular

14. A specific event can be called a _____ one.

no
rant (second or last)

15. Pronounce *warrant*. Does the a sound the same in both syllables war rant? _____ Which syllable has the unstressed vowel? _____

wAr rAnt

16. Though it is difficult to distinguish this vowel sound, you can remember it this way: wAr r___nt

warrant

17. A guarantee or written authorization is a _____.

last
a
mar dar lar

18. Three common and useful words having the same problems are *grammar, calendar,* and *similar*. First, look at the syllables: gram mar cal en dar sim i lar. The unstressed vowel appears in which syllable of each word? _____
What is the vowel? _____
Not only do these words have this similarity, they also have a graphic similarity: gram_____ calen_____ simi_____

grammar

19. From the Latin word *gramma*, meaning letter, comes the English word _____.

calendar

20. From the medieval Latin word *Kalendarium*, a money lender's account book, comes the English _____.

similar

21. To be related in appearance is to be sim_____.

a. calendar
b. grammar
c. similar

22. Supply each of these three words according to the context.

a. I have noted all my appointments on the _____.

b. Depending on the method of presentation, the study of _____ can be interesting.

c. The two plays have _____ plots.

last
iar (or liar)

23. *Familiar* and *peculiar* also have an unstressed vowel and a graphic similarity. Pronounce them. What same syllable in each word has the least stress, (first, second, last)? _____ What is the graphic similarity? _____

liar
iar

24. To be unusual or strange is to be pecu_____.
Common, or well-known is the definition of *famil*_____.

familiar
peculiar

25. We are now on a _____ road. He acts in a most _____ manner.

lar liar

26. Do not confuse these endings: simi_____ and fami_____.

last
e

27. Look at and then pronounce the word *sentence*. Which syllable has the unstressed vowel (first, last)? _____
Both the first and last syllables have which vowel? _____

sentences

28. A composition can be monotonous reading if all the s_____ are the same length.

REVIEW

a. *a a*   g. *lar*
b. *a*   h. *dar*
c. *iar*   i. *iar*
d. *i*   j. *o*
e. *a*   k. *e e*
f. *i*

29. Fill in the missing letters.

a. p__rticul__r   g. simi_____

b. gramm__r   h. calen_____

c. famil_____   i. pecul_____

d. r__diculous   j. __pinion

e. warr__nt   k. s__nt__nce

f. d__vide

mar dar lar
iar iar
ridiculous
divide
a a
a a
e e

30. Three words with similar endings are *gram_____, calen_____*, and *simi_____*.
Two words with similar endings are *famil_____* and *pecul_____*.
Two words with the same vowel sound in the first syllable are _____*diculous* and _____*vide*.
Three words having the same vowel in their first and last syllables are w__rr__nt, p__rticul__r, and s__nt__nce.

a a a da

31. An unstressed vowel in the middle of a word can often cause difficulties. Most of the problems are with the *i*, but some common and useful words have *e*, *o*, or *a* problems. Four with bothersome *a*'s are *separate*, *probably*, *comparative*, and *mandatory*. The words are syllabified like this: sep a rate, prob a bly, com par a tive, man da to ry. Pronounce them, noting the amount of stress placed on each syllable. Write the syllable of each word that has the unstressed vowel: _____ _____ _____ _____.

separate

32. If something is detached or disjointed it is sep_____.

separate

33. If the committees do not meet together, they hold *separate* _____ meetings.

probably

34. Most likely is the definition of the word *probably*.

probably

35. The storms will *probably* damage many houses.

mandatory

36. From the Latin *mandatum*, meaning a command, comes the word *manda*tory.

mandatory

37. Attendance at all lectures is *mandatory*.

third

38. Pronounce the word *comparative*. Although the two vowels in the middle of the word are the same, the unstressed *a* is in the (second, third) syllable. _____

comparative

39. If something can be estimated by comparison, it is said to be compar_____.

comparative

40. *Bigger* is the com_____ form of *big*.

a da a a

41. What are the missing letters in these words:
sep__rate   man____tory   prob__bly   compar__tive

second second
second second

42. Four common words often misspelled because of their *e* problem are *benefit*, *bulletin*, *category*, *mathematics*. Perform this operation mentally: say the words according to syllables, noting the amount of stress for each. In which syllable of *benefit* is the unstressed vowel? _____ in *bulletin*? _____ in *category*? _____ and in *mathematics*? _____

a. benefit
b. category
c. bulletin
d. mathematics

43. a. To be helpful or to improve is the definition of ben_____.

b. A class or a specifically designated division is called a cat_____.

c. A periodical published by an organization is sometimes called a bul_____.

d. The study of numbers and associated relationships is math_____.

a. bulletin
b. mathematics
c. category
d. benefit

44. Read these sentences for their meaning, then supply the correct "e" word for each.

a. How often does the company _____ come out?

b. What was your grade in the _____ course?

c. Do you intend to list all items in each _____?

d. A performance presented to raise money for charity is a _____.

second
o

45. Now let us turn to another group of words: *humorous, controversy, laboratory.* First pronounce them, dividing them into syllables. Which same syllable in each has the unstressed vowel (first, second, third)? _____
These words have which vowel problem? _____

a. humorous
b. controversy
c. laboratory

46. a. Laughable or comical is the definition of the adjective hu_____.

b. A dispute, especially a lengthy one, is a con_____versy.

c. A room equipped for scientific experimentation is a lab_____atory.

a. humorous
b. laboratory
c. controversy

47. Supply the correct "o" word for these sentences.

a. On our travels we saw many _____ sights.

b. My cousin works in a _____.

c. The new tax issue has started a _____ between the major political parties.

controversy
laboratory
humorous

48. A long dispute is a _____;
an experimentation room is a _____;
a comical picture is a _____ one.

REVIEW

49. Fill in the missing letters.

a. sep___rate

b. ben___fit

c. contr___versy

d. compar___tive

e. prob___bly

f. bull___tin

g. hum___rous

h. math___matics

i. mand___tory

j. lab___ratory

k. cat___gory

a. *a*
b. *e*
c. *o*
d. *a*
e. *a*
f. *e*
g. *o*
h. *e*
i. *a*
j. *o*
k. *e*

50. Let us turn to these words: *definite* and *dominant*. Here are two common words frequently used in writing and just as frequently misspelled. Look at, pronounce, and mentally syllabify both words. In which syllable is the unstressed vowel (first, second, third)? _____ Write the second syllable for each word: ____ ____

second
i i

51. To be specific is to be def_____; to be outstanding is to be dom_____.

definite
dominant

52. From the Latin *dominans* comes the English word _____; from the Latin *definire* comes the English _____.

dominant
definite

53. She had a _____ reason for arriving late.
specific

definite

54. Of all the characteristics attributed to the one cause, the last one is _____.
outstanding

dominant

55. The following four words are grouped together because they have a similar "rhythmic ring" and may be more easily remembered this way. Take *candidate* and *fascinate*. Each has three syllables. The major stress comes in which syllable of both words (first, second, third)? _____ The unstressed vowel is in which syllable of both words? _____ The vowel is ____.

first
second *i*

56. A person who seeks an office is a can____date. To spellbind or to attract irresistibly is the definition of *fas____ate*.

candidate
fascinate

57. Although his lack of education may prevent his being a _____, his ability to tell a story will
office-seeker
_____a wide audience.
attract

candidate
fascinate

third *i*

58. Two others with a rhythmic ring are *eliminate* and *legitimate*. Let us syllabify them first: e   lim   i   nate, le   git   i   mate. Which syllable in both has the unstressed vowel? _____ The troublesome vowel is _____.

legitimate eliminate

59. If something is lawful, it is le_____mate. If you wish to get rid of something, you want to elim___nate it.

legitimate

60. A solution that is based on logical reasoning or is a legal solution is a _____ solution.

eliminate

61. Stiff competition can _____ athletes from the preliminaries.

eliminated
legitimate

62. Sometimes an athlete can be _____ from a race by means that are not _____.

second (*ti*)
second (*i*)

63. Two words having similar endings can be presented together: *optimism* and *criticism*. Pronounce them carefully, listening to the stresses in each word. Of the three syllables in optimism, which has the unstressed vowel? _____ in criticism? _____

crit i cism
op ti mism

64. Now complete the last two syllables of each word: crit _____ _____   op _____ _____.

criticism
optimism

65. The act of making judgments is known as crit_____; tending to expect the best outcome is the definition of op_____.

criticism

66. To learn to write well one must be open to _____.

optimism

67. At times there may be more people who express pessimism than _____.

i second

68. The troublesome vowel in *dormitory* is again the ____. It is in the _____ syllable.

dormitory

69. From the Latin *dormitorium* comes the English word _____.

dormitory

70. A building to house a number of students can be called a _____.

third (*li*)

71. *Intelligence* is a common word and it is just as commonly misspelled, mainly because of its unstressed vowel. Pronounce the word and mentally divide it into syllables. In which syllable is the vowel to watch out for? _____

intelligence

intelligence

3
second
ri i

sacrifice
privilege

privileges
sacrifice

a. dominant
b. privilege
c. definite
d. candidate
e. legitimate
f. criticism
g. intelligence
h. fascinate
i. eliminate
j. optimism
k. dormitory
l. sacrifice

72. The ability to acquire and apply knowledge, and information or news received, are two definitions of the word intel_____.

73. The psychologist claims that Marty has superior _____.

74. And here are the last two words: *sacrifice* and *privilege*. Pronounce them, noting the syllables as you do. How many syllables does each have? _____ Both have the unstressed vowel in which syllable? _____
That syllable is sac_____fice and priv___lege.

75. To offer up something or to sell or give away at a loss is to sac_____; a special advantage or benefit can be called a priv_____.

76. Because the young ruler was not content with the _____s he already had, he was forced to _____ all his expensive possessions.

REVIEW

77. From the meaning of the sentence and other clues write these "vowel" words.

a. To be outstanding is to be dom_____.

b. A special advantage is a _____.

c. A specific proposal is a def_____ one.

d. Do you think the can_____ will continue to attract many voters?

e. A lawful course is a _____ one.

f. The book reviewer is known for his fair crit_____.

g. The ability to acquire and apply knowledge is called in_____.

h. His Irish brogue continues to fas_____ me.

i. How many words can you elim_____ without affecting the meaning?

j. No matter how serious the problem is, my grandfather believes that op_____ is the best attitude to have.

k. Are you living in the new dor_____?

l. Every winter the natives sac_____ their most productive animal.

POSTTEST

From the clues given below write the complete words.

1. ben_____   improve
2. dor_____   building to house students
3. ___pinion   conclusion or belief
4. sac_____   offering
5. pe_____   unusual or strange
6. sen_____   grammatical unit
7. hu_____   comical
8. def_____   specific
9. crit_____   judgments made
10. war_____   guarantee
11. lab_____   room for experimentation
12. can_____   office-seeker
13. ___diculous   silly or laughable
14. cal_____   table showing days of the year
15. prob_____   likely
16. bul_____   periodical
17. le_____   lawful
18. man_____   required
19. fam_____   well known
20. com_____tive   estimated by comparison
21. cat_____   designated division
22. dom_____   outstanding
23. ___vide   separate
24. gram_____   study of language
25. math_____   study of numbers
26. con_____versy   dispute
27. fas_____   attract
28. op_____   hopeful attitude
29. sep_____   detached or disjointed
30. priv_____   special advantage
31. sim_____   related
32. partic_____   specific
33. elim_____   get rid of
34. intel_____   information received, mental ability

Chapter 6

SOUND-ALIKE SUFFIXES

Is *able* correct, or is it *ible*? Should it be *ary* or *ery*, *ance* or *ence*? When suffix alternatives sound alike, how can you tell which one is right? As you know, questions like these arise daily, and without some forthcoming answers, it is difficult to spell words with these suffixes accurately. This chapter will help you answer these and similar questions. For some of these elements there are rules; for others, there are only tendencies for certain vowels or consonants to take this or that ending. But whether they are rules or tendencies, they will guide you to better spelling.

In this chapter you will learn to (1) apply rules or follow tendencies in the spelling of a number of useful words with suffixes; (2) practice and use these words in and out of context; (3) identify those words that do not follow rules or tendencies; and (4) from stated definitions, recognize and write the required words. In addition, this chapter will furnish a background needed for spelling other words with troublesome suffixes, and stimulate your curiosity about language in general.

PRETEST

Choose the correct ending for each of the following.

A. *able-ible*

1. permiss_____
2. accept_____
3. estim_____
4. change_____
5. admir_____

6. market_____
7. inevit_____
8. elig_____
9. consider_____
10. pass_____

11. poss_____

12. perish_____

13. defens_____

B. *ary-ery*

1. bound_____

2. station_____ (writing paper)

3. secret_____

4. libr_____

C. *ise-ize-yze*

1. adv_____

2. anal_____

3. critic_____

4. summar_____

5. surpr_____

D. *ance-ence (ant-ent)*

1. intellig_____ (ent, ant)

2. resist_____ (ance, ence)

3. equival_____ (ent, ant)

4. accid_____ (ant, ent)

5. defend_____ (ant, ent)

6. promin_____ (ance, ence)

7. exist_____ (ant, ent)

8. confid_____ (ence, ance)

9. sci_____ (ence, ance)

10. consequ_____ (ent, ant)

11. experi_____ (ence, ance)

12. magnific_____ (ence, ance)

14. repress_____

15. reduc_____

16. educ_____

5. cemet_____

6. Febru_____

7. contempor_____

8. station_____ (fixed)

6. emphas_____

7. paral_____

8. exerc_____

9. advert_____

10. real_____

13. mainten_____ (ance, ence)

14. excell_____ (ent, ant)

15. guid_____ (ance, ence)

16. influ_____ (ence, ance)

17. extravag_____ (ance, ence)

18. insist_____ (ent, ant)

19. attend_____ (ance, ence)

20. domin_____ (ant, ent)

21. preval_____ (ence, ance)

22. delinqu _____ (ant, ent)

23. brilli_____ (ance, ence)

24. signific_____ (ent, ant)

ABLE - IBLE

able
all are complete words
horr is just a base,
not a complete word

1. Generally, if the root is a full word it will take the suffix *able.* For example, *eat, drink,* and *read* are complete words, so they take *able:* eatable, drinkable, readable. Conversely, if the root is not a full word, it will usually take *ible.* In *permissible* and *possible* the bases are *permiss* and *poss.* Because they are not complete, the *ible* ending is correct. Which ending would the following take: *laugh   accept   lament   commend?* _____
State your reason briefly. _____

Why does *horrible* have *ible* and not *able?* _____

a. justifiable
b. playable
c. rectifiable
d. employable

2. Complete words ending in *y* preceded by a vowel also take *able.* For instance, *enjoy* ends in *oy,* so *enjoy* + *able* = *enjoyable.* Now take *rely.* It is also a complete word, but it ends in *y* preceded by a consonant (*l*). Usually words like *rely* change the *y* to *i* before a suffix beginning with a vowel, *rely* + *ed* = *relied.* Although *ible* also begins with a vowel, adding it to *reli* would produce a peculiar looking and sounding word ("unreliible"). So you must add *able: reliable.* Now add the suffix and write the complete words.

a. justify _____   c. rectify _____

b. play _____   d. employ _____

a. marketable
b. perishable
c. multipliable
d. comfortable
e. employable
f. variable
g. taxable
h. enjoyable
i. agreeable
j. pitiable

3. Apply what you have learned so far by choosing the correct suffix—*able* or *ible*—and writing the complete words.

a. market _____   f. vary _____

b. perish _____   g. tax _____

c. multiply _____   h. enjoy _____

d. comfort _____   i. agree _____

e. employ _____   j. pity _____

4. Another aid in choosing correctly between *able* and *ible* is to remember the related noun. Take a look at the two groups of words.

A.
commendation
consideration
admiration

B.
permission
admission
repression
perfection

ation
yes
ion
no
repress   perfect
both

What is the five-letter ending of each in group A? _____
Is the part of each word before this five-letter ending complete? (Remember that "silent e" words usually drop the e before a suffix beginning with a vowel.) _____
What is the three-letter ending of each word in group B? _____

Is the part before this ending complete in each word? ____
Name the complete word(s) in Group B. _____

The double s in the words in group B appears in (complete, incomplete, or both) words.

complete
ss

5. Even though there are only a few words in the above lists, we can point out some tendencies. The two nounal endings are important: *ation, ion*. The words in group A (*ation*) have (complete, incomplete) words within them? _____

The words in group B (*ion*) are either complete or incomplete. The incomplete words have what double letter in the base? ____

able
ible
ible

6. Here are the same nouns as well as the *able-ible* adjectives relating to them.

A.

commendation	commendable
consideration	considerable
admiration	admirable

B.

permission	permissible
admission	admissible
repression	repressible
perfection	perfectible

Again, we can make some generalizations (not rules, you notice).
If a noun is formed by adding *ation,* the adjective will probably be formed by adding (*able, ible*). _____
If *ion* is the ending for the noun, the ending for the adjective will undoubtedly be (*able, ible*). _____
Whether in a complete or incomplete word, the double s will usually take (*able, ible*). _____

a

7. An exception to the "completeness" idea for *able* is the word evitable, and its negative *inevitable*, derived from the Latin verb *evitare*, meaning to avoid. Very often the spelling of the original word governs the spelling of the English derivative. Look carefully at the ending of the Latin verb. Which letter tells you to add *able* or *ible* to the incomplete forms *evit* and *inevit*? ____

evitable
inevitable

complete
do
do not
repression

ion

a. kissable
b. passable
c. repressible

no
no
yes

able

a. responsible
b. dispensable
c. defensible

8. Now write these two exceptions:
_____ and _____.

9. Look at these words: *kiss, pass,* and *repress.*
All are (complete, incomplete) words. _____
All (do, do not) have an *ss.* _____
All (do, do not) have a related noun ending in *ion.* _____
Name the related noun(s). _____

10. *Repress* has a double *s* and a related *ion* noun, so it takes *ible* to form the adjective. *Kiss* and *pass* do not have related nouns ending in *ion,* so they take *able.* Before adding *able* or *ible* to a word having *ss,* you must first determine if that word has a related noun ending in _____.

11. Form the adjectives from these words by adding *able* or *ible:*

a. kiss _____   b. pass _____   c. repress _____

12. In addition to the double *s,* an *ns* at the end of a base can alert you to add *ible.* But again you should determine if there is a related noun and what its ending is. Here are three bases:
defens   respons   dispens
Is there a related noun for *defens?* _____
How about *respons?* _____
And *dispens?* _____

13. Because *defens* and *respons* do not have related nouns, they will follow the general tendency for *ns* to take *ible.* The related noun for *dispens* is *dispensation.* Which ending will the adjective take (*able, ible*)?_____

14. Form the adjectives by choosing *able* or *ible.*

a. respons_____   b. dispens_____   c. defens_____

15. On page 74 is a list of words to which you can add *ation* or *ion* to form the related noun and then *able* or *ible* to form the adjective. Apply what you have learned so far and complete the words for both columns. If no word is appropriate write "none." Watch the "silent e" words as the e is usually dropped before the vowel suffix.

a. destruction
destructible
b. none
passable
c. imagination
imaginable
d. corruption
corruptible
e. accession
accessible
f. admission
admissible
g. consolation
consolable
h. none
inevitable
i. perfection
perfectible
j. dispensation
dispensable

Root or base	Noun	Adjective
a. destruct	_____	_____
b. pass	_____	_____
c. imagine	_____	_____
d. corrupt	_____	_____
e. access	_____	_____
f. admiss	_____	_____
g. console	_____	_____
h. inevit	_____	_____
i. perfect	_____	_____
j. dispens	_____	_____

a. S
b. S
c. S
d. H
e. H
f. H
g. S
h. S

16. The sound of c and g at the end of a complete word or a base can also suggest the correct ending.
The soft sound of c is like an s (as in *city*).
The hard sound of c is like a k (as in *category*).
The hard sound of g is like the g in *go* or *get*.
Pronounce the words below and identify by S or H if the italicized portions are soft or hard sounds.

a. peace _____   e. drag _____
b. change _____   f. destruction _____
c. reduce _____   g. eligible _____
d. educate _____   h. lace _____

soft
ce
able
able
g (no e)
hard
able

17. Look at and pronounce these two groups of words.

A.   B.

legible   revocable
serviceable   educable
noticeable
enforceable
changeable

Group A.
What sound of c or g do you have here? _____
Each word with the soft c has what two-letter ending before the suffix? _____
Each word with ce takes (*able, ible*). _____
The word with ge at the end of the root takes (*able, ible*).

_____

The word with the soft g and suffix *ible* has (g, ge) as its ending? _____

Group B.
What sound of c do you have here? _____
What ending does each word have? _____

able
ible
able
able

18. Using just a few words from the same list as illustrations, let us develop some generalizations.

legible   serviceable
changeable   educable

Words having a soft g in ge at the end of the root word take (*able, ible*). _____
Those having a soft g at the end of the base take (*able, ible*). _____
Those having a soft c in ce at the end of the root word take (*able, ible*). _____
Those having a hard c take (*able, ible*). _____

a. serviceable
b. educable
c. eligible
d. enforceable
e. changeable
f. legible
g. revocable
h. reducible
i. deducible

19. Pronounce these *able-ible* words, look at the ending of the bases, then write the complete word.

a. service_____   f. leg_____
b. educ_____   g. revoc_____
c. elig_____   h. reduc_____
d. enforce_____   i. deduc_____
e. change_____

REVIEW

able

20. Generally, full or complete words, like *commend* or *market*, take (*able, ible*). _____

a. *able*
b. *able*

21. Which ending (*able, ible*) would you add to
a. complete words ending in y, like *enjoy?* _____
b. complete words ending in y, like *comply?* _____

change y to i

22. In adding *able* to *comply*, you must first _____.

able

23. Generally, words ending in ce or ge (like *service* or *change*) take (*able, ible*)? _____

a. soft
b. *ible*
c. there is no ce or
   ge—just c and g

24. In your mind add the *able-ible* ending to these bases and pronounce them as complete words: leg_____ reduc_____

a. Each has the (soft, hard) sound of c or g? _____

b. Each takes (*able*, *ible*)? _____

c. Why did you choose this ending? _____

_____

a. remissible
b. perfectible
c. dispensable
d. corruptible
e. revocable
f. consolable
g. admissible
h. irritable

25. Look at the endings of these nouns and then write the related adjectives.

a. remission _____ e. revocation _____

b. perfection _____ f. consolation _____

c. dispensation _____ g. admission _____

d. corruption _____ h. irritation _____

evitable
inevitable

26. Finish the spelling by adding *able* or *ible*.
evit_____ inevit_____

ible

27. The consonants *ns*, as in *defens* and *respons* take (*able*, *ible*)? _____

able

28. Because *dispens* has the related noun dispensation, the *ns* takes (*able*, *ible*)? _____

noun ending in *ation*
so adjective is *able*;
the c is hard

29. Look at and pronounce these two nouns: *education, revocation.*
Give two reasons why *educable* and *revocable* take *able*.

_____

_____

a. accession
   accessible
b. irritation
   irritable
c. impression
   impressible
d. consideration
   considerable
e. digestion
   digestible
f. none
   creditable
g. detestation
   detestable
h. variation
   variable
i. none
   understandable

30. For the following complete and incomplete words write (1) the related noun (if none, write "none") and (2) the correct *able-ible* adjective.

Root or base	Noun	Adjective
a. access	_____	_____
b. irritate	_____	_____
c. impress	_____	_____
d. consider	_____	_____
e. digest	_____	_____
f. credit	_____	_____
g. detest	_____	_____
h. vary	_____	_____
i. understand	_____	_____

a. serviceable
b. eligible
c. permissible
d. reducible
e. inevitable
f. changeable
g. educable
h. horrible
i. responsible
j. despicable

31. Complete these with *able* or *ible.*

a. service_____   f. change_____

b. elig_____   g. educ_____

c. permiss_____   h. horr_____

d. reduc_____   i. respons_____

e. inevit_____   j. despic_____

ARY - ERY

ery

32. Definition and association of ideas can often help you remember whether the ending is *ary* or *ery*. For example, writing paper is called *stationery*. If you hesitate in spelling this word, remember that it has the same ending as pape*r*.
Another commonly misspelled word can be remembered by its definition. A corpse is usually buried in a grav<u>e</u> and the site for many grav<u>es</u> is called a graveyard, or cemet_____.

cemetery
stationery

33. Complete these definitions:
A place for burying the dead is a cem_____; writing paper is called sta_____.

a. stationery
b. cemetery

34. Complete these sentences:

a. For thank-you notes, Susie bought pink _____.

b. Michael helped put in tombstones at the _____.

boundary
library
secretary
February
contemporary

35. Because *stationery* and *cemetery* are the two commonly misspelled *ery* words, complete the spelling of the following:

bound_____   Febru_____

libr_____   contempor_____

secret_____

contemporary
library
February
boundary
secretary
stationary

36. The word meaning modern or present day is *contem* _____.
A place where books are deposited is a li_____.
The second month of the year is Feb_____.
A limit is a bound_____.
A person who types and takes shorthand can be called a secre_____.
A seat that is not movable is station_____.

stationary

37. If writing paper is *stationery*, the word meaning fixed, not movable, is _____.

a. boundary
b. stationary
c. library
d. contemporary
e. secretary
f. February

38. Now write the words that match the definitions.

a. limit   _____

b. fixed   _____

c. book depository   _____

d. present day   _____

e. one who types _____

f. second month   _____

REVIEW

paper

39. To spell *stationery* correctly, what word do you associate with it? _____

e

40. What one vowel goes in each blank? c__m__t__ry

ary

41. You always end the name of the second month with *ary* or *ery*? _____

secretary

42. Someone who types and takes dictation is a _____.

ISE - IZE - YZE

surprise
arise
exercise

43. It is not the purpose here to supply the derivations of words ending in *ise, ize,* or *yze.* Suffice it to say that many come from Old French and Latin, hence *ise*; and many come from the Greek, hence *ize* and *yze.* Because of their common origin, the "ise" words are grouped together and because association helps you to remember, the words will be related in what can be called "association sentences."
Here is the first:
It should be no *surprise* that I *exercise* when I *arise.*
There are two words with two syllables:

_____   _____

The third has three: _____

r
2

44. *Surprise* and *exercise* are often misspelled in other parts of the words as well. For example, what consonant appears twice in the first word? _____
In the second syllable of the second word are there (2 or 3) letters? _____

surprise
exercise

45. To fill with wonder or disbelief is the meaning of *sur*_____. *To practice* means to ex_____.

arise

46. The word to get up is a_____.

a. surprise
b. exercise
c. arise

47. Read the sentences below and supply the three words just studied.

a. He will _____ us all some day.

b. Athletes must _____ every day to keep fit.

c. I _____ at six-thirty.

surprise
exercise
arise

48. Now back to our original sentence:
It should be no _____ that I_____ when I _____.

advise
enterprise
supervise
advertise
merchandise

49. Let us put some *ise* words into a business setting:
Investing in an *enterprise* may mean having to *advise* and *supervise* a number of employees, and to *advertise* the *merchandise*.
The one word with two syllables is _____.
The rest have three syllables each:

_____   _____

_____   _____

enterprise
supervise
advertise
merchandise

50. A business venture is called an enter_____.
To direct or inspect is to super_____. To make a public announcement is to ad_____. Goods or wares are known as mer_____.

enterprise
advise
supervise
advertise
merchandise

51. Let us return to our original sentence: Investing in an _____ may mean having to _____ and _____ a number of employees, and to _____ the _____.

yze

52. Now look at this group of words.

realize   criticize
emphasize   characterize
recognize   summarize
analyze   paralyze

Of the eight words above, only two have which ending (*ize, yze*)? _____

analyze
paralyze

53. To separate a whole into its parts and examine them is the meaning of *anal*_____; to render ineffective, or to unnerve is the meaning of *paral*_____.

analyze
paralyze

54. These two words are similar in another respect:
an____yze   par____yze

a. paralyze
b. analyze

55. Supply the correct *yze* word:

a. Some forms of polio will _____ an individual.

b. To reach an effective solution you should first _____
the problem.

analyze paralyze

56. The two words ending in yze are _____
and _____.

re al ize
em pha size

57. For the "ize" words let us continue "association sentences." Two go nicely together:
Did you *realize* you didn't *emphasize* the right points in
your argument? Here is the first syllable for each—you
write the rest.
re _____ _____   em _____ _____

realize
emphasize

58. To understand clearly, or to accomplish is to
re_____. To stress or to achieve is to em_____.

a. realize
b. emphasize
c. realize

59. Write the correct *ize* word:

a. I do _____ what you are saying.

b. You should _____ your main points.

c. Some day he may _____ his dream.

realize
emphasize

60. To return to our original sentence: Did you _____
that you didn't _____ the right points in your
argument?

3
rec og nize
crit i cize

61. Here is our next sentence:
Even though you *recognize* his faults, you don't need to
criticize him publicly.
Each word has ____ syllables. Complete the syllables for
each:
rec _____ _____   crit _____ _____

recognize
criticize

62. To take notice is to rec_____.
To judge or evaluate is to crit_____.

criticize

63. Of these two words which one often carries the idea
of simply finding fault? _____

recognize

64. If you are aware that you have seen certain people
before, you _____ them.

recognize
criticize

summarize
characterize

characterize
summarize

a. characterize
b. summarize
c. characterize

65. Even though you _____their faults, you don't have to _____ them publicly.

66. The last two important words are *summar*_____ and *character*_____.

67. To describe the qualities of or give character to is the definition of the word _____.
To sum or to restate briefly is to _____.

68. Write the correct one of these two for each sentence.

a. His temper and his bad manners _____ him as a boor.

b. Now _____ your main ideas.

c. How would you _____ Mr. Jones?

REVIEW

a. ize	i. ize
b. yze	j. ise
c. ise	k. ize
d. ize	l. ise
e. ise	m. yze
f. ise	n. ise
g. ize	o. ise
h. ise	p. ize

69. Choose the correct ending *ize-yze-ise* for these words:

a. real_____   i. character_____

b. anal_____   j. merchand_____

c. advert_____   k. recogn_____

d. emphas_____   l. exerc_____

e. surpr_____   m. paral_____

f. adv_____   n. superv_____

g. critic_____   o. ar_____

h. enterpr_____   p. summar_____

ANCE - ENCE

existence
insistence
consistence
persistence
competence

70. There are no rules to guide you in adding the suffixes *ance* (*ant*) or *ence* (*ent*). Certain consonants, however, tend to take the *a* or the *e*. The consonants *t* and *v* tend toward the *a*: accept—acceptance; import—importance; relev—relevance. But some *t*'s do not:
exist   insist   consist   persist   compet
If accept, import, and relev take *ance*, add the correct ending to the five exceptions, and write the complete words:

_____   _____

_____   _____

_____

existence
competence
insistence
consistence
persistence

71. Association can help you to remember these exceptions.
First you must exist, so you have exist_____. Last, you have sufficiency or compet_____. In between are the various stages of striving:
_ _sist_____   _ _ _sist_____   _ _ _sist_____

existence
insistence
consistence
persistence
competence

72. Name these five exceptions.

_____   _____
_____   _____
_____

a. relevant
b. importance
c. insistent
d. resistance
e. competent
f. assistance
g. existent
h. acceptance
i. persistence
j. admittance
k. repentant
l. inheritance

73. Now apply what you have learned so far and add the correct suffix.

a. relev   (ant, ent)   _____

b. import   (ance, ence)   _____

c. insist   (ant, ent)   _____

d. resist   (ance, ence)   _____

e. compet   (ent, ant)   _____

f. assist   (ance, ence)   _____

g. exist   (ent, ant)   _____

h. accept   (ance, ence)   _____

i. persist   (ence, ance)   _____

j. admitt   (ance, ence)   _____

k. repent   (ant, ent)   _____

l. inherit   (ance, ence)   _____

a. S   d. S
b. H   e. H
c. S   f. S

74. The sound of the c and g will often govern which ending is correct. The hard sound of c (as in cat) and the hard sound of g (as in go) require *ance* or *ant*. The soft sound of c (as in city) and the soft sound of g (as in gem) take *ence* or *ent*.
Pronounce these words; then identify which sound each underlined consonant has. Use S (soft) or H (hard).

a. adolescent   _____   d. magnificent   _____

b. extravagance   _____   e. significance   _____

c. intelligence   _____   f. emergence   _____

ance
ent
ence

75. Look again at the list above.
The words with the hard c or g have which ending? _____
The words with the soft c have which ending? _____
The words with the soft g have which ending? _____

a. **emergence**
b. adolescent
c. extravagance
d. intelligent
e. significance
f. magnificent

76. Complete the spelling of these.

a. emerg_____ (*ance, ence*) _____

b. adolesc_____ (*ent, ant*) _____

c. extravag_____ (*ance, ence*) _____

d. intellig_____ (*ent, ant*) _____

e. signific_____ (*ance, ence*) _____

f. magnific_____ (*ant, ent*) _____

REVIEW

a. intelligence
b. existence
c. important
d. insistence
e. acceptance
f. assistant
g. persistence
h. extravagant
i. consistency

77. Test your skill by adding the correct suffix and writing the complete word.

a. intellig_____ (*ance, ence*) _____

b. exist_____ (*ence, ance*) _____

c. import_____ (*ent, ant*) _____

d. insist_____ (*ence, ance*) _____

e. accept_____ (*ence, ance*) _____

f. assist_____ (*ent, ant*) _____

g. persist_____ (*ence, ance*) _____

h. extravag_____ (*ant, ent*) _____

i. consist_____ (*ancy, ency*) _____

ence
ance

78. Now look at these words carefully:

equivalent   eminence
excellence   imminence
prevalent   prominence
                    permanent

Both groups have *ence* or *ent*. In the first the consonant *l* precedes the ending and in the second it is *n*. But look at these: *balance, dominance, maintenance*. Here you also have *l* and *n* preceding the suffix, but it is *ance*, not *ence*. The two groups of words illustrates the tendency of *l* and *n* to take _____. The three exceptions take _____.

balance dominance
maintenance

79. What are the three exceptions?

_____ _____ _____

a. ence   e. ance
b. ance   f. ence
c. ence   g. ence
d. ence   h. ance

80. Supply the correct suffix: *ance* or *ence*.

a. equival_____   e. bal_____

b. domin_____   f. perman_____

c. emin_____   g. immin_____

d. preval_____   h. mainten_____

a. excellence
b. equivalent
c. prevalent
d. balance
e. maintenance
f. eminent
g. permanent

81. Complete the word for each sentence.

a. In striving for excell_____ you must
ence, ance
work hard.

b. Equal in substance or value is the meaning of
equival_____.
ant, ent

c. To be widespread is to be preval_____.
ant, ent

d. There should be bal_____ of power.
ence, ance

e. The state of keeping in proper condition is called
mainten_____.
ance, ence

f. A renowned person is emin_____.
ant, ent

g. Lasting is the definition of perman_____.
ant, ent

abundance
attendance
guidance
defendant

82. The consonant *d* tends to take the same endings as
the consonants *l* and *n*. There are times, however, when
it does not, and it is these "do nots" that are troublesome.
From the list below choose the "do nots" and write them.

superintendent   antecedent
accident   independence
abundance   dependent
attendance   guidance
confidence   defendant

_____

_____

_____

defendant
guidance
attendance
abundance

83. Let us try combining to better remember them: The
defend_____ needs guid_____. A large attend_____
suggests an abund_____.

a. defendant
b. superintendent
c. guidance
d. attendant
e. accidence
f. confidence
g. dependent
h. abundance
i. incident

84. Keeping these exceptions in mind, fill in the correct suffix.

a. defend_____ (ant, ent)

b. superintend_____ (ant, ent)

c. guid_____ (ance, ence)

d. attend_____ (ant, ent)

e. accid_____ (ence, ance)

f. confid_____ (ence, ance)

g. depend_____ (ant, ent)

h. abund_____ (ance, ence)

i. incid_____ (ant, ent)

i
flu
qu

85. Look carefully at these groups.

A.	B.	C.
experience	influence	delinquent
convenience	affluence	consequent
ingredient		
science		

There is a single letter or two or more letters that are responsible for the *ence* or *ent* ending.
In group A what vowel is responsible?_____
In group B what two consonants plus a vowel are responsible? _____
In group C what consonant and a vowel are responsible?
_____

i flu
qu

86. In other words, the endings *ence* or *ent* usually follow the single vowel _____, the three letters _____, and the two letters _____.

ance ant

87. One "i" word does not take the usual ending. Complete its spelling: brilli_____ or brilli_____.

brilliant
brilliance

88. To be full of light is to be _____; the extreme brightness or splendor is called _____.

a. delinquent
b. influence
c. brilliant
d. ingredient
e. consequently
f. science

89. Read each sentence and complete the spelling of each.

a. To neglect or fail to do is to be delin_____.

b. His mother has a lot of influ_____ on him.

c. Bob has been called a brilli_____ student.

d. The cook scolded the apprentice for leaving out an ingredi_____.

e. It is raining; consequ_____ly I won't go.

f. Nancy has won a scholarship in sci_____.

ence

90. Words having *flu* and *qu* have which ending (*ance*, *ence*)? _____

exceptions

91. Would the following words illustrate the usual tendency of *d* or are they exceptions? _____

abundance   defendant

attendance   guidance

no—it is an exception

92. Is the word *brilliant* a good example of the usual tendency of *i*? _____

ence

93. The consonants *l* and *n* tend to take which ending (*ance*, *ence*)? _____

ance   ance
ance

94. Complete the endings.

bal_____   domin_____

mainten_____

consist
persist
compet

95. The consonant *t* and *v* tend to take *ance*. The word *exist* is an exception, so is *insist*. Name the other three words (or bases) that are exceptions. _____

_____   _____

a. *ance*
b. *ance*
c. *ance*
d. *ance*

96. Choose the correct ending (*ance*, *ence*).

a. resist_____   c. import_____

b. relev_____   d. assist_____

g and c are hard
and require ance

97. State why *extravagance* and *significance* have *ance* and not *ence*.

_____

ence
each has a soft c
or g

98. Which ending (*ance*, *ence*) would you add to these words:

emerg_____   intellig_____   adolesc_____

magnific_____

State your reason briefly. _____

_____

a. defendant
b. guidance
c. abundance (ant)
d. dominance (ant)

99. From each twosome, choose one that takes *ance* or *ant*.

a. defend_____ depend_____

b. confid_____ guid_____

c. accid_____ abund_____

d. domin _____ anteced_____

POSTTEST

Supply the correct ending for each of the following.

A. ary-ery

1. contempor_____
2. station_____ (fixed)
3. bound_____
4. cemet_____

5. Febru_____
6. secret_____
7. libr_____
8. station_____ (paper)

B. ise-ize-yze

1. ar_____
2. superv_____
3. character_____
4. anal_____
5. surpr_____
6. recogn_____

7. adv_____
8. exerc_____
9. critic_____
10. paral_____
11. real_____
12. summar_____

C. able-ible

1. multipli_____
2. enforce_____
3. perfect_____
4. enjoy_____
5. admiss_____
6. respons_____
7. commend_____
8. leg_____

9. corrupt_____
10. revoc_____
11. kiss_____
12. horr_____
13. consol_____
14. irrit_____
15. intellig_____
16. dispens_____

D. ance-ence (ant-ent)

1. sci_____ (ence, ance)

2. conveni_____ (ence, ance)

3. **depend_____ (ant, ent)**

4. import_____ (ence, ance)

5. domin_____ (ence, ance)

6. extravag_____ (ent, ant)

7. abund_____ (ance, ence)

8. resist_____ (ance, ence)

9. persist_____ (ence, ance)

10. attend_____ (ance, ence)

11. bal_____ (ence, ance)

12. adolesc_____ (ent, ant)

13. signific_____ (ance, ence)

14. delinqu_____ (ent, ant)

15. compet_____ (ent, ant)

16. defend_____ (ant, ent)

17. mainten_____ (ance, ence)

18. relev_____ (ent, ant)

19. excell_____ (ence, ance)

20. brilli_____ (ant, ent)

21. perman_____ (ant, ent)

22. guid_____ (ance, ence)

23. afflu_____ (ant, ent)

24. emerg_____ (ence, ance)

Test
PART ONE

A. Add the correct endings and write the complete words.

ance-ence

1. exist_____
2. relev_____
3. depend_____
4. adolesc_____
5. experi_____
6. mainten_____
7. persist_____
8. insist_____

9. intellig_____
10. magnific_____
11. consequ_____
12. conveni_____
13. compet_____
14. domin_____
15. confid_____

able-ible

16. destruct_____
17. change_____
18. admiss_____
19. employ_____
20. rely_____
21. notice_____
22. elig_____
23. corrupt_____

24. dispens_____
25. respons_____
26. poss_____
27. commend_____
28. educ_____
29. irrit_____
30. imagine_____

ary-ery

31. cream_____
32. diction_____
33. cemet_____
34. station_____ (paper)
35. contempor_____

36. bound_____
37. secret_____
38. custom_____
39. station_____ (fixed)
40. libr_____

ise-ize-yze

41. recogn_____

42. ar_____

43. real_____

44. paral_____

45. adv_____

46. emphas_____

47. critic_____

48. advert_____

49. surpr_____

50. anal_____

B. Fill in the missing prefix *(per, pre, pro, de, dis)*. Be sure to check the meanings of the words in the right-hand column.

51. Nancy recently received a _____motion. (advancement)

52. In his twenty-first year, John Mill was in a complete state of _____spair. (state of hopelessness)

53. Three teachers were granted _____mission to travel to China. (consent)

54. Two of the children have a contagious _____ease. (illness)

55. Joe is responsible only for those tasks that _____ tain to his job. (belong to)

56. The earthquake and fire _____stroyed every building in the downtown area. (demolished)

57. The actor's _____formance was outstanding. (act)

58. What have you _____cided to do? (concluded)

59. The doctor cannot _____scribe a drug that will cure the illness. (give rules, directions)

60. New techniques show the _____gress in science. (forward course)

61. Six of the seven _____jects were approved. (proposals)

62. The boys in the front row tried to _____tract the speaker. (divert attention)

63. When it is hot, Bill _____spires a lot. (sweat)

64. The store owner will _____credit the thieves' story. (cast doubt on)

65. The weather bureau's _____dictions came true. (foretelling)

66. A student should always read the _____face of a book. (introduction)

67. The brothers have a _____pensity for disobeying traffic laws. (inclination)

68. Several governmental documents have been _____ classified from "secret" to "confidential." (downgraded)

69. Officers often have to _____arm criminals.   (take away
weapons)

70. Aunt Sarah had several _____sentiments of the car   (foreboding)
accident.

C. In the following sentences the words in italics are sometimes spelled correctly and sometimes not. If correct, write a C in the blank and if incorrect, spell the word accurately.

71. She has no *defenite* plans.   _____

72. *Separate* the clothes into three bundles.   _____

73. You should improve your *grammer*.   _____

74. The results of the flood are *disastrous*.   _____

75. The lodge can *accomodate* us for a week.   _____

76. The agent is extremely *agressive*.   _____

77. The youngest child acts *peculiarly*.   _____

78. The second month of the year is *February*.   _____

79. Mother bought a new *vacume* cleaner.   _____

80. The posts are *parallel*.   _____

81. Yesterday Sue had a high *temperture*.   _____

82. In Shakespeare's *Othello,* Iago is the *villain*.   _____

83. I have *accummulated* many books.   _____

84. Please *reccomend* two more books.   _____

85. It was a dreadful state of *lonliness*.   _____

86. Three times the *lightening* struck.   _____

87. The structure of the two novels is *similar*.   _____

88. I did not see a *familiar* face in the crowd.   _____

89. Your actions do not *warrent* a pardon.   _____

90. At times we must *sacrifice* a great deal.   _____

91. Grandmother gave me her watch as a *remembrance*.   _____

92. Cindy is a *mischievious* little girl.   _____

93. Tomorrow I will *aquire* two lakeshore lots.   _____

94. The band has good balance but not much *rythm*.   _____

95. All the business courses are *unnecessary*.   _____

96. Why must there be *predjudice* in the world?   _____

97. They often *embarass* me. _____

98. I *attest* to their loyalty. _____

99. Jack said it was a *priveledge* to meet me. _____

100. She studied her *psychology* for three hours. _____

Part Two
MEANING
AND SPELLING

Chapter 7

THE "SEED" ROOTS

Because the roots *sede*, *cede*, and *ceed* are pronounced alike ("seed"), they must be distinguished by another means, their meaning. And so in this chapter you will concentrate on the meaning of these roots as well as on the meaning of various prefixes to be attached to these roots, and practice spelling a number of useful words. By the end of the chapter you will combine the right prefix with the right root and understand the reasons for your choice. Also, by learning the meanings of the prefixes included in this chapter you will be able to choose the correct prefix for other words.

PRETEST

A. Fill in the blanks with the appropriate ending:

ceed, sede, cede

1. ac_____
2. pro_____
3. con_____
4. se_____

5. ex_____
6. suc_____
7. ante_____
8. re_____

9. super_____
10. inter_____

B. Fill in the appropriate prefix.

11. To replace is to _____sede.

12. To yield consent is to _____cede.

13. To advance is to _____ceed.

14. To go before is to _____cede.

15. To follow after in time or order is to _____ceed.

16. To settle differences is to ____cede.

17. To go beyond is to _____ceed.

18. To withdraw from a political group is to _____cede.

19. To yield strongly or to admit is to _____cede.

20. To go back is to _____cede.

a. cede   e. cede
b. ceed   f. ceed
c. cede   g. cede
d. ceed   h. sede

1. Word endings that sound like "seed" are easy to learn as there are only three: sede   cede   ceed. The sede ending has only one prefix combined with it: super. The ceed ending has only three: pro, ex, suc. The cede ending takes other prefixes.
For the following prefixes attach the correct root.

a. con_____   e. ac_____

b. pro_____   f. ex_____

c. pre_____   g. inter_____

d. suc_____   h. super_____

supersede

2. Super means over or above. Combining this prefix with the root that comes from the Latin sedere, meaning to sit, produces the word meaning that which sits above or over, in other words, replaces it. That word is _____.

it has sede in it

3. How does this Latin verb sedere govern the spelling of the English derivative? _____

supersede

4. The word that means to "sit over or above" or to replace is _____.

pro
ex
suc
suc

5. Three words have a different ending—ceed—which comes from the Latin cedere, meaning to go. The prefix pro means forward, and ex means beyond.
If you go forward, you _____ceed.
If you go beyond, you _____ceed.
   The prefix suc is a variant of sub, which means under, next, or following after.
If you go next (follow after in order), you _____ceed.
Succeed also means to attain a desired end. If you get to your goal, you _____ceed.

a. proceed
b. exceed
c. succeeds
d. exceed
e. proceed
f. succeed

6. Read the sentences for their meaning, then write the correct "seed" word for each.
a. Why can't the meeting _____?
b. Drew realized he was going to _____ the speed limit.
c. At the next meeting club members will decide who _____ Joe Casey as president.
d. The demand for strawberries will _____ the supply.
e. Now you can _____ with the next part of the examination.
f. You must work diligently if you want to _____.

exceed proceed
succeed

7. What three words end in ceed?

_____ _____ _____

supersede

8. Name the only word ending in *sede*.

_____

cede

9. The rest of the "seed" words must end in (*sede*, *cede*, *ceed*). _____

cede

10. The third ending which also comes from the Latin *cedere*, meaning to go or to withdraw, constitutes a complete word, meaning to surrender possession formally, usually rights or territory. If a country formally gives up some of its possessions, it is said to _____ them.

cede

11. Some countries have been forced to _____ parts of their territories.

precede

12. Prefixes can be combined with this root to form quite a few words. For instance, adding *pre*, which means before, gives you the word _____.

before

13. If Henry precedes Jack, he goes _____ him.
before, after

precede

14. If you tell an anecdote before you begin your main speech, this anecdote will _____ the speech.

recede

15. Let us try another with the same root. The prefix *re* means back. To go back would be to _____.

recede

16. The tidal waters will _____ in about an hour.

precede
recede

17. To go before is to _____; to go back is to _____.

a. accede
b. concede

18. The prefix *ac* (a variant of *ad*) means to, so with this root it forms *accede*, meaning to go to, or to yield consent. *Con* in *concede* is an intensive, so this word has a strong meaning of yielding (for example, a privilege or a right) or of admitting.
Write the appropriate word in each sentence.

a. The members of the minority party will eventually _____ to the wishes of the majority.

b. After a bitter conflict, the senator agreed to _____ to the committee's demands.

concede

19. Which word has the stronger sense of yielding: *accede, concede?* _____

a. accede
b. concede

20. Read the sentences first to decide which has the stronger sense of yielding, then write the correct word.

a. Joe urged his brother to _____ to his supervisor's wishes.

b. I doubt that Don Hardy will ever _____ his voting rights.

a. 4
b. 2
c. 3
d. 5
e. 1

21. Now match these words with their definitions.

a. cede   1. to go before   _____

b. accede   2. to yield consent   _____

c. recede   3. to go back   _____

d. concede   4. to surrender   _____

e. precede   5. to yield a right   _____

a. cede   e. cede
b. ceed   f. cede
c. sede   g. ceed
d. ceed   h. cede

22. Complete these words.

a. ac_____   e. con_____

b. ex_____   f. pre_____

c. super_____   g. suc_____

d. pro_____   h. re_____

intercede

23. *Inter* means between or among. If you go between two persons, say to settle a quarrel, you inter_____.

antecedes

24. *Ante* means to precede in time or space. An event that goes before another in time _____ it.

antecedes

25. The First World War _____ the Second World War.

intercede

26. To act between parties to settle differences is to _____.

recede

27. The weather bureau predicted that the river would reach its crest and then would start to _____.

between

28. To intercede is to go _____.

a. ante
b. inter
c. pro
d. ex

29. Read the sentences for their meaning, then choose the correct prefix for each root: *ac pre ante inter pro ex con*

a. A person's ancestors are called _____cedents.

b. Since the members have reached a deadlock, I hope that an arbitration board will _____cede soon.

c. Let us _____ceed with the meeting.

d. The supply will _____ceed the demand.

REVIEW

supersede

30. Write the word ending in *sede*. _____

exceed proceed
succeed

31. What words end in *ceed*? _____

_____

a. ceed   f. cede
b. cede   g. cede
c. sede   h. ceed
d. ceed   i. cede
e. cede   j. cede

32. Finish the spelling.

a. suc_____   f. con_____

b. inter_____   g. pre_____

c. super_____   h. pro_____

d. ex_____   i. retro_____

e. ac_____   j. ante_____

secede

33. The Latin *se* meaning away or apart can be combined with the root that comes from the Latin *cedere*, meaning to go. If a state would "go away" from the Union it would _____ from the Union.

a. away (apart)
b. back
c. beyond
d. before
e. forward
f. next
g. above
h. between

34. Supply the correct prefix meanings.

a. To secede is to go _____.

b. To recede is to go _____.

c. To exceed is to go _____.

d. To precede is to go _____.

e. To proceed is to go _____.

f. To succeed is to come _____ in order.

g. To supersede means to sit over or _____.

h. To intercede is to act _____.

proceed
precede

35. The word meaning to go forward is _____; the word meaning to go before, or in front of, is _____.

a. precede
b. proceed
c. supersede

36. The following words are misspelled. Write the words correctly.

a. preceed   _____

b. procede   _____

c. supercede   _____

POSTTEST

A. Fill in the blanks with the appropriate "seed" ending.

1. re_____   5. ac_____   9. suc_____

2. ex_____   6. pro_____   10. ante_____

3. pre_____   7. super_____

4. con_____   8. se_____

B. Read the sentences carefully, then write the correct "seed" word for each.

11. The eldest son will _____ his father as president.

12. When the road is cleared, the parade will _____ up the street.

13. The water will _____ by tomorrow.

14. John will _____ to the desires of his friend.

15. If Mary stands in front of Jack in the ticket line, she will _____ him.

16. As the age of automation continues, new methods of production and management will _____ the old.
           replace

17. If you are not careful, you will _____ the limit.

18. The workers asked for a mediator to _____ in the dispute.
                           act between

19. To strongly yield consent is the definition of the word _____.

20. You must work diligently if you want to _____.

Chapter 8

HOMONYMS

Homonyms are words that sound exactly alike but differ in spelling and meaning. A spelling error occurs when one homonym is substituted for another. For instance, if you use *principle*, meaning a rule or law, for *principal*, meaning a head of a group, you will produce a confusing sentence, not only momentarily puzzling your reader, but undoubtedly irking him as well. The homonyms included in this chapter are those that cause a great deal of difficulty. But by the time you finish the chapter, you will have no difficulty with them. The main objective of this chapter is to provide you with sufficient material concerning the meanings and the parts of speech of these homonyms so that you can readily choose between them, not only according to their definitions but also in the context of sentences. Also, by working diligently with these homonyms, you can form a basis for learning other pairs (or sets) of words identical in sound.

PRETEST

Choose the correct homonyms for these sentences.

1. The president of the firm paid me a high _____.
   complement, compliment

2. I placed the book _____.
   their, there, they're

3. We are _____ too late.
   all ready, already

4. The dog wagged _____ tail.
   it's, its

5. Burlap is a _____ material.
   course, coarse

6. What is your _____ reason?

principle, principal

7. The recommendation was made by members of the _____.

council, counsel

8. He is _____ correct.

all together, altogether

9. Did you buy any _____?

stationery, stationary

10. I am meeting Judge Doe in his office at the state _____.

capital, capitol

11. For your report you must _____ two references.

sight, cite, site

12. He _____ directly in front of us.

past, passed

13. Mary wants to go _____.

to, too

14. The well is on _____ property.

their, there

15. How far is the _____ for the new hospital from here?

sight, site

16. It was a _____ performance!

capitol, capital

a. already
b. all ready

1 Two expressions that are used interchangeably when they should not be are *all ready* and *already*. Besides being different in the number of words, they have different meanings. *All ready* is an adjective phrase meaning quite or completely ready. *Already* is an adverb meaning at or by this time.
Write the appropriate expression.

a. The best tickets were _____ sold.

b. We are _____ to go to the lake.

all ready
already

2. The expression meaning quite or completely ready is _____; the one meaning at or by this time is _____.

a. all ready
b. already

3. Choose the correct homonym: *all ready, already.*

a. By noon the soldiers were _____ to move to the front.

b. By the time we arrived, John had _____ gone.

2 2

1 1

all together
altogether

everyone in a group
on the whole,
completely,
thoroughly

a. altogether
b. altogether
c. all together

2

informal

all right

all right

4. The expression meaning completely or quite ready has how many words _____ and how many *l*'s _____?

5. The expression meaning at or by this time has how many words _____ and how many *l*'s _____?

6. *All together* and *altogether* are another pair. The two-word expression concentrates on the *all*—everyone in a group—whereas the single word has meanings of completely, on the whole, or thoroughly. Which expression is correct for each sentence: After the storm the farmer found the animals huddled _____. I am _____ certain that he lied.

7. Write the correct meaning(s) for each expression.
all together _____
altogether _____

8. Choose the correct expression: *all together, altogether.*

a. The assumption is _____ false.

b. The critics said the performance was _____ entertaining.

c. To win a lasting peace, nations must work _____.

9. Here is a controversial pair: *all right* and *alright*. For some time the one-word expression has been considered (and still is by some) a misspelling of the two words, meaning satisfactory or correct. Today *alright* is accepted as an alternative form, but usually in informal writing only. The one way you can always be right is to spell this expression as _____ word(s).

10. Alright is accepted by some but only in (formal, informal) writing. _____

11. Which form is always correct? _____

12. Choose the expression that is correct in all styles of writing:
His responses to the panel's inquiries were _____.
alright   all right

building

13. Although *capital* and *capitol* are easily confused, they are just as easy to use correctly. *Capitol* (with an o) is the building in which a state legislature meets, a building that usually has a dome on top. *Capitol* (with a capital C) refers to the building in Washington, D.C., where Congress meets. *Capital* (with an a) is used in contexts which demand other meanings than the _____ where a legislature assembles.

capitol
Capitol

14. The state legislature assembles at the _____ and the Congress of the U.S. occupies the _____ in Washington, D.C.

capital

15. If you remember that *capitol* relates to a building, then it is easy to use *capital* correctly for other meanings. For example, the major city or town of a state is called a _____.

capital

16. Lima is the _____ of Peru.

capital

17. This word also has the meaning of first-rate or excellent: It was a _____ performance.

capital

18. Or, the meaning of a stock of wealth. To buy the franchise, the grocer needed a great deal of _____.

a. Capitol
   capital
b. capitol
   Capitol
   capital

19. Choose the correct one: *capital, Capitol, capitol*

a. To finance my trip to the _____ in Washton, D.C. I need more _____.

b. When referring to the building where a state legislature meets you write _____; to the building where Congress meets _____; and to the major city of a state _____.

a. principal
b. principal
c. principles
d. principal

20. The nouns *principle* and *principal* are easy to distinguish. *Principle* is a noun only and refers to basic truths, laws, or rules. *Principal* can be either an adjective meaning chief or main, or a noun referring to a leader, or a sum of money. Choose the correct homonym.

a. The head of a school is a _____.

b. He cited three _____ reasons.

c. The community recognized the governor as a person of high _____s.

d. A sum of money on which interest is calculated is _____.

noun
wrong (incorrect)

21. The word principle is not correct in this phrase "a principle reason" because it can be used only as a _____, not as an adjective. Also the meaning is _____ for this context.

principle

22. The noun referring to basic truths, laws, or rules is _____.

a. principle
b. principal
principal
principles
c. principal

23. Choose the correct homonym: *principal, principle.*

a. Some people live only according to the _____ of self-preservation.

b. The _____ reason Mr. Brown was appointed _____ of Stock High School is that he has high _____.

c. Lindsay's account totaled $1,000, of which approximately $900 was the _____.

a. stationary
b. stationery

24. *Stationery* and *stationary* are another good pair to learn. *Stationery* is a noun, meaning either the paper you write on or the establishment that sells it and related items. *Stationary* is an adjective meaning fixed, not movable. Write the appropriate word.

a. The group remained _____.

b. My mother bought me some _____.

stationary
stationery

25. The adjective meaning fixed is _____; the noun meaning writing paper is _____.

stationery

26. The last syllable of the word *paper* contains er, and so do the last syllables of the word for writing paper: _____.

noun

27. In this sentence—The architect suggested putting in stationary seats—the word *stationery* cannot be substituted because the sentence needs the adjective to modify seats, and *stationery* is always a _____.

stationery

28. Mavis wrote to me on her best _____.

stationary

29. The rows of seats in the auditorium are _____.

a. coarse
b. course
c. coarse
d. course
e. course

30. The adjective *coarse* cannot be substituted for the noun *course*. *Coarse*, meaning inferior in quality, crude, or harsh, is always an adjective. *Course*, on the other hand, can be used as a noun or verb, but never as an adjective. As a noun, it means a direction, route, or onward movement; as a verb it means to follow a direction.
Supply the correct word.

a. Burlap is a _____ material.

b. He follows a definite _____.

c. The clerk has _____ manners.

d. We followed the _____ of the stream.

e. Rivers _____.

coarse

31. Although his manners were _____, he had an engaging personality.

course

32. Fads usually run their _____ in a short time.
course, coarse

coarse
course
verb

33. Whereas _____ is always an adjective, _____ is either a noun or a _____.

a. site
b. sight
c. cite
d. sight
e. sight

34. *Site*, *cite*, and *sight* are homonyms to watch out for. *Site* is always a noun and means a place of location or an event. *Cite* is always a verb, meaning to mention or quote as an authority. *Sight* can be used as a noun or a verb. As a noun it can mean one's vision, a field of vision, or a spectacle; as a verb, it means to aim.
Choose the correct homonym.

a. Orchard Gardens is the _____ for a new development project.

b. Soon the sailor will _____ land.

c. The politician will _____ many authorities to refute the argument.

d. He should _____ his target at any minute.

e. Suddenly it came into _____.

site
noun
cite
verb
noun
sight

35. The word meaning a place of location _____ is always a _____.
noun, verb
The word meaning to mention or quote an authority _____ is always a _____.
The third homonym can mean to take aim, as a verb, or a view or spectacle as a _____. This word is _____.

a. cite
b. sight
c. site
d. sighted

36. Choose one for these sentences: *cite site sight*

a. Did you _____ Forster's theory?

b. The Grand Canyon is a breathtaking _____.

c. We came around the curve and then saw the _____ for the plant.

d. He raised his rifle and carefully _____ his target.

REVIEW

a. capitol
b. course
c. all ready
d. stationery
e. principal
f. cite
g. altogether
h. already
i. site
j. coarse

37. Now test your skill by writing the correct homonyms.

a. I drove to the _____ in twenty minutes.

   state legislature building

b. Richard has decided on a definite _____ of

   coarse, course

action.

c. When the whistle blew, the workers were _____

   already, all ready

to leave.

d. Jane received two boxes of _____.

   stationary, stationery

e. The speaker emphasized the _____

   principal, principle

points strongly.

f. He did not _____ sufficient evidence to

   site, cite, sight

win.

g. Her behavior is _____ proper.

   altogether, all together

h. By the time Joe arrived, his brother had _____

   all ready, already

_____ left.

i. My uncle picked a _____ in the country for

   sight, site

his new house.

j. Shoppers often choose a _____ material

   course, coarse

for drapes.

a. P e. P
b. C f. C
c. P g. P
d. C h. C

38. Contractions are not to be mistaken for possessives. Contractions are identified by an apostrophe which stands for an omitted letter. For example, the ' in it's stands for the omitted i in the verb: it is. The possessive its never has an apostrophe. Identify by P or C whether these words are possessives or contractions.

a. their _____ e. whose _____

b. who's _____ f. it's _____

c. its _____ g. your _____

d. you're _____ h. they're _____

who is
it is
you are
they are

39. In the contractions the apostrophe stands for the beginning letter of a verb. What is it in who's? _____ in it's? _____ in you're? _____ in they're? _____

a. who's
b. you're
c. its
d. their

40. Choose the correct words.

a. Do you know _____ going to the dance?
who's, whose

b. Tell me when _____ ready.
your, you're

c. We watched the mother bird feed _____ young.
it's, its

d. They did not like _____ seats downstairs.
they're, their

They're
there
their

41. A word sounding exactly like their and they're is there. It is an adverb meaning in or at that place: I placed the package over there. Write the correct word—there, their, they're, in these related sentences.
Nancy shouted, "_____ here."
"Where?" I replied. "Over _____," she said, "waving _____ hands."

a. too
b. two
c. to
d. to
e. too

42. These words also sound alike but differ in meaning and spelling: to too two. The word two pertains to the number 2. To (with one o) can be a preposition, as in to the store, or it can help to form an infinitive, as in to go home. Too (with two o's) is an adverb meaning also or more than enough: I want to go too, or It is too much.
Fill in the correct homonyms below.

a. Do you want a cone _____?

b. I received a _____ dollar raise.

c. Mary went downtown _____ buy a robe.

d. Don't bother about giving a present _____ me.

e. There is _____ much noise.

two
too
to

43. The numeral is _____; the adverb is _____; the preposition or part of an infinitive is _____.

a. too
b. two
c. to
d. too

44. Choose the correct homonym: *to, too, two.*

a. I, _____, was offered a job there.

b. The typist gets _____ dollars an hour.

c. Don't give it _____ her.

d. We had _____ many problems to worry about Jim's ball game.

verb

45. You need never confuse *know* and *no* because *know* is a verb meaning to perceive, or to be certain of, and *no* is either an adjective "no bananas are left," or an adverb, "he is no better than I."
In this sentence—How do you know he is over twenty—you cannot use *no* because it is an adverb or an adjective, and the sentence requires a _____.

a. know
b. no
c. no
d. know

46. Write *know* or *no* below.

a. I don't _____ the instructor.

b. He is _____ better than he appears to be.

c. I looked, but there were _____ strawberries on the counter.

d. How do you _____ the speaker is right?

no know

47. The word that means none as an adjective and not as an adverb is _____. The word that sounds like it but is a verb is _____.

passed—sentence
needs a verb

48. *Passed* and *past* should present no problem as *passed* is simply the past tense (*ed*) of the verb *pass:* He passed in front of me. *Past* can be either a noun: a distinguished *past*, an adjective: in *past* years, or an adverb: walked *past* the store. In this sentence—He _____ me on the street—which homonym is correct and why?

_____

past

49. Of the two, *passed* and *past*, which one can be either a noun, adjective, or adverb? _____

a. passed
b. past
c. past
passed

50. Write *passed* or *past* for these sentences.

a. The train _____ within 20 feet.

b. He thanked us for _____ favors.

c. In the _____ the Johnsons have _____ us on the street without any sign of recognition.

---

a. yes
b. meaning is wrong
—need verb meaning
praise

51. Although both *compliment* and *complement* are nouns and verbs, they have such different meanings that they should never be confused. A *compliment* is an expression of praise, and *to compliment* is to praise someone. A *complement* is something that completes and *to complement* is to complete.

a. Is the homonym used correctly in this sentence: The new complement of soldiers arrived today. _____

b. Why won't *complement* fit this sentence: He continued to compliment me for my fine work. _____

---

a. compliment
compliment
b. complemented
c. complement
complimented

52. Write in *complement* or *compliment*.

a. I waited for him to _____ me, but when the _____ came, it dripped with sarcasm.

b. In finishing the design, Mrs. White _____ the rows of red figures with a row of blue ones.

c. When the fresh _____ of soldiers arrived, the general _____ them on their appearance.

---

a. council is a noun,
it means a group
b. yes
c. counsel

53. The last group is *council, counsel,* and *consul.* All three are nouns. A *council* is a deliberative body (like a city council, for example). *Counsel* means either a lawyer or a group of lawyers giving advice, or the advice itself. *Consul* refers to an officer in the foreign service of his country. *Counsel* can also be a verb, to give advice or to recommend.

a. In this sentence—He tried to _____ me about going to college—*council* would be incorrect. State two reasons why. _____

b. Is the correct homonym used here: He offered his counsel. _____

c. Whereas *council* and *consul* are nouns only, _____ can be either a noun or a verb.

a. council
counsel
consul
b. council counsel
consul

counsel

a. counsel
b. complement
c. their
d. to
e. its
f. passed
g. know no
h. You're
i. too
j. Who's
k. compliments

54. Choose the correct word: *counsel, council, consul.*

a. A deliberative assembly is a _____; a lawyer who conducts a case in court is called _____; and an officer in the foreign service is a _____.

b. The student _____ sought _____ from the French _____.

55. Which word is not only a noun? _____

REVIEW

56. Test your skill in choosing the correct homonym.

a. My adviser tried to _____ me about enter-
$\quad$council, counsel
ing the contest.

b. The new _____ of soldiers saved
$\quad$compliment, complement
the fortress.

c. The couple insisted that we were going to camp on
_____ property.
there, their

d. He decided not to give the money _____ the
$\quad$to, two, too
church.

e. Minnesota is known for _____ lakes.
$\quad$it's, its

f. As we neared the reviewing stand, Mike _____
$\quad$past, passed
us on the left.

g. Many inhabitants _____ _____ other way
$\quad$know, no$\quad$know, no
of life.

h. Jim gasped, "_____ going."
$\quad$Your, You're

i. I want to go _____.
$\quad$two, to, too

j. _____ driving to school?
$\quad$Whose, Who's

k. Lorraine received many _____
$\quad$compliments, complements
for her fine portrayal of Anna.

POSTTEST

Write the correct homonym for each sentence.

1. The ruler suggested that a new _____ of militia be added.
   compliment, complement

2. Don't you know _____ meaning?
   it's, its

3. He has a distinguished _____.
   past, passed

4. Do you plan to take a specific _____?
   coarse, course

5. They huddled _____ in the barn.
   altogether, all together

6. How are you going to _____ _____ him?
   council, counsel

7. It was a thrilling _____.
   cite, sight, site

8. The auditorium seats are _____.
   stationery, stationary

9. My uncle works at the _____ in Washington, D.C.
   capitol, capital, Capitol

10. Please give the dress _____ Doris.
    to, two, too

11. By the time we arrived he had _____ gone.
    all ready, already

12. The mother bird fed _____ young.
    its, it's

13. A foreign service officer is a _____.
    counsel, consul

14. _____ not going to the picnic.
    Their, There, They're

15. _____ magazine is this?
    Whose, Who's

16. The officer is a person of high _____.
    principal, principle

Chapter 9

SIMILAR WORDS

Words that are similar in appearance or sound can also be confused. For example, the pairs, *accept-except,* and *affect-effect,* are used interchangeably when they should not be. By noting differences in spelling, sound, and particularly meaning, you can quickly eliminate any hesitation in choosing the right word of such a pair, or set, as the case may be. The objectives of this chapter are therefore these: you will distinguish between alternatives by their meaning and spelling; you will practice spelling and using a number of these similar words, and you will establish a *modus operandi* for spelling other confusing words.

PRETEST

Choose the correct word for each sentence.

1. This has been _____ a day.
   quite, quiet

2. Do you have _____ to the storeroom?
   excess, access

3. I'm afraid I will _____ my place in line.
   loose, lose

4. His remarks were _____.
   causal, casual

5. Can you _____ what will happen?
   prophecy, prophesy

6. Please _____ my apologies.
   except, accept

7. She is taller _____ I.
   then, than

8. Do you expect any bad _____ from the new drug?
   affects, effects

9. Do a _____ job.
   through, thorough

10. Can you _____ the storm?
    whether, weather

11. I listened patiently to the complaints of the _____.
    personal, personnel

12. He cannot _____ me.
    advice, advise

13. Lucy tripped on the _____ floor board.
    lose, loose

---

a. access
b. excess
c. access

1. Access is a noun meaning a way of approaching or a right to enter. *Excess,* also a noun, means the act of going beyond, or exceeding. Since both words are nouns, you must choose according to the meaning. Which one is correct in these sentences?

a. He has _____ to the vault.

b. There is an _____ of potatoes.

c. We have direct _____ to the stage.

access
excess

2. The word signifying a means of nearing is _____ ; the word meaning the act of going beyond is _____ .

a. excess
b. access
c. access

3. Choose the correct word: *access, excess.*

a. What shall we do about the _____ of basketballs?

b. How do you gain _____ to the wing of the building?

c. Because the boy's parents did not accompany him, he was refused _____.

way of nearing
act of going beyond

4. Access means _____.
Excess means _____.

No. Causal pertains to a cause. Sentence demands "unconcerned."

5. In the two adjectives *casual* and *causal* watch the placement of the *s* and *u.* The word that pertains to a cause would be *causal;* the word that means occurring by chance, aimless, or unconcerned is *casual.* Is the underlined word used correctly here? If not, why not?
He has a <u>causal</u> appearance.

_____
_____

causal

a. casual
b. causal
casual
c. casual

6. The adjective that refers to a cause is _____.

7. Choose the correct word: *casual, causal.*

a. He has a _____ manner.

b. To prove his argument he must show _____ relationships, not _____ ones.

c. Because he had no time for preparation, he could offer only some _____ remarks.

---

unconcerned,
aimless, occurring
by chance
relating to a cause
yes in each case

8. Define *casual:* _____

Define *causal:* _____

9. *Affect* is a verb meaning to change or to alter. It is never a noun. *Effect*, on the other hand, is both a noun and a verb. As a noun it means a result; as a verb to bring about a result, or to accomplish. Are the underlined words used correctly in these sentences?

a. What will the effect be?

b. How do the legislators expect to effect the changes in the new law?

c. The car accident affected his hearing.

---

affect
effect

10. The verb meaning to change or alter is _____.
The verb meaning to accomplish or bring about a result is _____.

a. affect
b. effects
c. effect

11. Choose the correct word: *affect, effect.*

a. The new housing bill will _____ many people.

b. What major _____s do you expect?

c. Can the school system _____ the changes without more money?

verb
alter, change
result
bring about a result,
accomplish

12. *Affect* is always a _____ and means to _____.
Effect as a noun means _____; as a verb it means _____.

prophecy

13. *Prophecy* and *prophesy* are easy to distinguish. First, *prophecy* is the noun and *prophesy* is the verb. Second, *to prophesy* is to predict, and what is predicted is the *prophecy*. Which word is correct for this sentence:
He stated that his _____ would come true.

prophesy

14. Which word is the verb: *prophecy* or *prophesy?*

_____

prophecies

15. All were astounded by her _____.
prophesies, prophecies

prophesy

16. He demanded time to _____ but he was refused.

to predict
the prediction

17. Prophesy means _____.
Prophecy means _____.

a. Yes
b. Yes

18. The verb *accept* means to receive, to take willingly. It should not be confused with *except*, meaning other than or with the exclusion of. Check whether the underlined word is correct.

a. Everyone <u>except</u> Joe went home.
Yes _____ No _____

b. We will <u>accept</u> the offer.
Yes _____ No _____

receive
other than, with the
exclusion of

19. *Accept* means _____.
Except means _____.

a. except
b. accepts
c. except

20. Choose the correct word: *except, accept.*

a. All the bottles _____ _____ one broke.

b. Everyone _____s Grandma Smith as a friend.

c. All went to the picnic _____ Mac.

advise (the verb)

21. *Advise* (with an *s*) is a verb meaning to counsel; *advice* (with a *c*) is a noun meaning the counsel given. Which word is appropriate here:
What did he _____ you to do?

advise
advice

22. The counselor offered to _____ the students,
advise, advice
but he knew they would not accept his _____.
advice, advise

advise
advice

23. The verb meaning to counsel is _____; the noun meaning the counsel given is _____.

to counsel
the counsel given

24. Advise means _____.
Advice means _____.

(1) Sentence needs a verb. (2) Loose has the wrong meaning—context demands meaning of mislay.

25. *Lose* and *loose* differ in three ways. *Lose* is a verb; *loose* is an adjective. *Lose* means to mislay, to be deprived of; *loose* means free, not fastened down tight. *Lose* has one o; *loose* has two.

Name two reasons why *loose* cannot be used in this sentence: I always lose my gloves.

_____

_____

a. loose
b. lose
c. lose
d. lose

26. Select the correct word: *lose, loose.*

a. The bolt is _____.

b. If Tim is not careful, he will _____ his cap.

c. Don't _____ your balance.

d. So that you will not _____ any more time, take the bus.

adjective—free
verb—to mislay

27. *Loose* is an _____, meaning _____.
Lose is a _____, meaning _____.

quite quiet

28. *Quite* and *quiet* differ in spelling, meaning, and pronunciation. *Quite* has one syllable; *quiet* has two. *Quite* is an adverb meaning rather, actually, or completely. *Quiet* is an adjective meaning silent, away from noise. Combine these two words into a phrase meaning rather still:

_____

quite

29. Today is _____ hot for June.
quiet, quite

cold

30. Since *quite* is an adverb, it modifies what word in this sentence: It is quite cold. _____

quiet

31. After ten o'clock the park is _____.

adjective
silent
adverb
rather, completely, actually

32. *Quiet* is an _____ and means _____.
Quite is an _____ and means _____.

REVIEW

a. advice
b. effects
c. prophecy
d. lose

33. Test your skill by selecting the correct words.

a. Whose _____ will you take?
advice, advise

e. affect
f. quiet
g. accepted
h. access
i. causal

b. Don't expect too many good _____ from
the new bill.
affects, effects

c. Many a _____ has come true.
prophecy, prophesy

d. If you say yes, you may _____ your privileges.
lose, loose

e. Jack's actions will _____ all of us.
affect, effect

f. There is a _____ zone around the hospital.
quite, quiet

g. His defeat was _____ good-naturedly.
accepted, excepted

h. The corridor offers good _____ to all the
music studios.
excess, access

i. He lost his argument by stating false _____
relationships.
casual, causal

a. than
b. then

34. *Then* means at that time in the past: I was six then;
or next in time or space: I will go to the store; then I will
go downtown. *Than* relates to a statement showing comparison: Mary is more agile than Betty; or a preference:
I would rather dance than eat.
Write the correct word for each sentence.

a. He is younger _____ I am.

b. He was younger _____.

then refers to time
and space—than re-
fers to a preference

35. In this sentence—I would rather dance than play golf
—why can't you use *then?* _____

time and space
a comparison, a
preference

36. The adverb *then* refers to _____.
The conjunction *than* refers to a _____
or a _____.

a. than
b. then
c. than

37. Choose the correct word: *then, than.*

a. He writes better _____ I do.

b. If she practices hard for the next half hour, _____
she can play outdoors.

c. I would prefer exercising on the machine rather _____
jogging for ten minutes.

a. through
b. thorough
c. through

38. *Through* and *thorough* are like *quite* and *quiet* in that one word has one syllable and the other two. *Through*, the one-syllable word, is a preposition which means by way of, to the end, to finish successfully. *Thorough*, the two-syllable word, is an adjective meaning complete, or painstakingly accurate.
Write the correct word for each sentence.

a. I got my information _____ Jane.

b. He did a _____ job.

c. I saw the performance _____.

thorough
through

39. The adjective meaning finished and accurate is _____. The preposition meaning by way of, to the end, or finish successfully is _____.

a. to the end
b. by way of
c. finish successfully

40. What is the meaning of *through* in these sentences?

a. The critic saw the opera through. _____

b. It was through John that we found out. _____

c. I got through the examination. _____

a. painstakingly accurate
b. complete

41. What does *thorough* mean here?

a. Josie is a thorough worker. _____

b. He listened with thorough enjoyment. _____

personnel

42. Now take *personal* and *personnel*. *Personal* is an adjective and pertains to something done to or for a person. *Personnel* is a noun referring to a body of persons employed or active in an organization. Which word is correct here?

The supervisor spoke to the _____.

personal
personnel

43. The adjective referring to a person is _____;
the noun referring to people employed at an office is _____.

a. personal
b. personnel
c. personal
d. personnel

44. Choose the correct word: *personal, personnel.*

a. He resigned for _____ reasons.

b. The factory _____ want a representative to discuss their needs.

c. After hearing the cases, the judge said that most of the complaints were _____.

d. The adjective *personal* cannot be substituted for the noun _____.

a person
a body of persons
at a company

45. *Personal* refers to _____.
Personnel refers to _____.

a. weather
b. whether
c. weather

46. Although *weather* and *whether* sound almost alike, they differ in all other respects. *Weather* is a noun that means atmospheric conditions, or a verb that means to expose to these conditions or to pass through an ordeal safely. *Whether* is a conjunction which introduces the first of two or more alternatives. Choose the correct word for each sentence.

a. We will have cold _____ soon.

b. It does not matter _____ we sit or stand.

c. I cannot _____ many more snowstorms.

whether

47. The word that introduces an alternative is (*weather*, *whether*). _____

verb

48. *Whether* is a conjunction, but *weather* serves either as a noun or as a _____.

whether
weather

49. The result of the debate matters not; what is important is _____ Tony can _____
             whether, weather   whether, weather
the long and tiring ordeal.

REVIEW

a. through
b. personnel
c. weather
d. than
e. whether
f. then

50. Choose the correct word for each sentence.
a. When you are _____ with the pamph-
             thorough, through
let, return it to me.

b. The administrator spoke to all the _____.
             personal, personnel

c. The forecast for tomorrow's _____ is
             weather, whether
rain.

d. Mr. Park owns more property _____ Mr. Stone.
             then, than

e. Don't ask me _____ I can go or not.
             whether, weather

f. Complete this assignment; _____ do the next.
             then, than

POSTTEST

Write the correct word(s) for each sentence.

1. You cannot make noise in the _____ zone.
   quite, quiet

2. We must know _____ the school is open.
   whether, weather

3. Please do me a _____ favor.
   personal, personnel

4. I hope the _____ boards have been fixed.
   lose, loose

5. The supply of ironing boards is in _____ of those needed.
   excess, access

6. To win your argument you must show _____ relationships.
   casual, causal

7. Everyone _____ Larry as a friend.
   accepts, excepts

8. We don't know what the _____ of his speech will be.
   effects, affects

9. The _____ came true.
   prophesy, prophecy

10. There are times when legislation is the only way to _____ the
    affect, effect

necessary changes.

11. When you finish this chapter, _____ begin the next.
    then, than

12. It's a question _____ I would rather dine out or stay home.
    weather, whether

13. What _____ will you give him tomorrow?
    advise, advice

Test
PART TWO

A. Select the correct "seed" word for each sentence: *accede concede recede proceed precede supersede exceed succeed intercede secede*

1. The tidal waters will _____.

2. The factions need a mediator to _____ in the dispute.

3. It is rumored that a Southern state wants to _____ from the Union.

4. Complete pages 1 and 2, then _____ to page 3.

5. Reluctantly will I _____ that his claims are true.

6. A good speaker will often _____ a speech with an anecdote.

7. The new model will certainly _____ the earlier ones.

8. Although he has failed repeatedly, he finally managed to _____.

9. The plant manager announced he would _____ to the workers' requests.

10. Some drivers knowingly _____ the speed limit.

B. Choose the correct word in each set and write it in the blank.

11. What _____ will Jerry's ten absences from his English class have on his grade? (effect, affect)

12. Our club will go to Chicago _____ it snows or not. (weather, whether)

13. Abby needs more _____ to start her gift shop. (capital, capitol)

14. I think that skating is more fun _____ bowling. (then, than)

15. Yesterday three members of the _____ resigned. (council, counsel)

16. In her new position, Mary will _____ her clientele what investments to make. (advice, advise)

17. If the workers strike, they could _____ their job rights.   (lose, loose)

18. Mr. Thomas said that ill health was the _____ _____ reason for resigning.   (principle, principal)

19. How many times has he _____ my house?   (passed, past)

20. The shoes were _____ expensive to buy.   (to, two, too)

21. The beagle wagged _____ tail.   (it's its)

22. Debbie will enroll in a business _____.   (coarse, course)

23. It is difficult to _____ which plan to adopt.   (know, no)

24. Mr. Manet is the new French _____.   (council, consul)

25. _____ going to the dance?   (Whose, Who's)

26. When I arrived home, Jim had _____ gone.   (all ready, already)

27. The visiting anthropologist will address the _____ _____ of the Midas Corporation.   (personnel, personal)

28. Don Brown was unwilling to _____ the advice of his superiors.   (accept, except)

29. From my window I can see the dome of the _____ _____.   (capital, capitol)

30. Put the trunks over _____.   (their, there)

31. Please listen to his _____.   (prophecy, prophesy)

32. Don't take any _____ baggage.   (access, excess)

33. Their everyday attire is _____.   (causal, casual)

34. She expected them to _____ her.   (complement, compliment)

35. Forest Hills is a beautiful _____ for a ranch.   (cite, site, sight)

Part Three
RULES
AND SPELLING

Chapter 10

DOUBLING THE FINAL CONSONANT

Knowing when to double the final consonant and when not to will help you to spell many words correctly. In this chapter you will not only learn several rules about doubling in words of one or more syllables, but you will also apply them to many words. Also you will learn to immediately recognize words that do not follow the doubling rule, words that do and do not double depending on the shift in stress when a suffix is added, and a few exceptions to the rules. By the end of the chapter you will not be misspelling *occurrence*, *transferring*, or other words requiring the final consonant to be doubled, nor will you be misspelling words that do not double the final consonant.

PRETEST

Add the specified suffixes to the following words.

1.	plan	*er*	_____	14.	gossip	*y*	_____
2.	wit	*y*	_____	15.	instill	*ing*	_____
3.	streak	*ed*	_____	16.	equip	*ed*	_____
4.	plug	*er*	_____	17.	omit	*ed*	_____
5.	tax	*ing*	_____	18.	dim	*er*	_____
6.	exploit	*er*	_____	19.	excel	*ent*	_____
7.	drop	*ed*	_____	20.	confer	*ence*	_____
8.	begin	*ing*	_____	21.	benefit	*ed*	_____
9.	occur	*ence*	_____	22.	chagrin	*ed*	_____
10.	dim	*ly*	_____	23.	vex	*ing*	_____
11.	repeal	*ed*	_____	24.	delight	*ful*	_____
12.	transfer	*ing*	_____	25.	traffic	*er*	_____
13.	propel	*ant*	_____				

c. d. f. g. h.
. . . .
b. c. e. f. h.

1. One-syllable words ending in a single consonant preceded by a single vowel double the final consonant before adding a suffix beginning with a vowel (or the suffix y). For instance, the word cup ends in a single consonant (p) preceded by a single vowel (u). If you add the suffix ed (which begins with the vowel e) you double the consonant: cupped. But if you add the suffix ful (which begins with the consonant f) you do not double the p: cupful. Let us look at the words link and peel. Link ends in two consonants (nk) and peel in a consonant preceded by two vowels (eel), so these words do not meet the requirements.

One consonant cannot be doubled even though it is preceded by a vowel. This consonant—x—has a ks sound and is treated as two consonants. Take the word tax as an example; pronounce it slowly and you will hear the ks sound. If you add ed to tax you would spell it: taxed.

In the one-syllable words below identify those that end in a single consonant preceded by a single vowel.

a. hail	d. club	g. bug
b. drill	e. pack	h. rip
c. mop	f. tap	

. . . .

Identify the suffixes that would require doubling.

a. *ment*	d. *ly*	g. *ful*
b. *ing*	e. *y*	h. *ance*
c. *er*	f. *ed*	

a. chatty
e. dimmed
f. clammy
g. fretting

2. Pick out each combination of a word and a suffix to which this doubling rule applies, add the specified suffix, and write the complete word. If the rule does not apply to a combination, leave the space blank.

a. chat	y	_chatty_
b. streak	ed	_streaked_
c. farm	er	_farmer_
d. tax	ing	_taxing_
e. dim	ed	_dimmed_
f. clam	y	_clammy_
g. fret	ing	_fretting_
h. burn	er	_burner_

BuRned BuRneR

b. stooped
d. fretful
e. taxed
f. pealing
h. grimly

3. If a particular word or suffix does not meet the requirements of this rule, you can assume that the final consonant is not doubled before the suffix. Choose the combinations below to which this rule does *not* apply, add the specified suffix, and write the complete words.

a. bar   ed   *barred*

b. stoop   ed   *stooped*

c. stop   ed   *stopped*

d. fret   ful   *fretful*

e. tax   ed   *taxed*

f. peal   ing   *pealing*

g. chub   y   *chubby*

h. grim   ly   *grimly*

a. planner
b. droplet
c. restful
d. clubs
e. dimmer
f. speared
g. shrieking
h. plugged
i. skinny
j. dimly
k. vexing
l. dropped

4. Now test your skill by writing complete words for all the combinations.

a. plan   er   *planner*

b. drop   let   *droplet*

c. rest   ful   *restful*

d. club   s   *clubs*

e. dim   er   *dimmer*

f. spear   ed   *speared*

g. shriek   ing   *shrieking*

h. plug   ed   *plugged*

i. skin   y   *skinny*

j. dim   ly   *dimly*

k. vex   ing   *vexing*

l. drop   ed   *dropped*

REVIEW

c. d. f.

5. Which factors must be considered in the doubling of the final consonant in a one-syllable word?

a. it must end in a single vowel

b. it must end in a single consonant preceded by a single consonant

c. it must end in a single consonant preceded by a single vowel

d. it must not end in the consonant *x*

e. the suffix begins with a consonant

f. the suffix begins with a vowel or is the suffix *y*

last *f* is preceded by another *f* (consonant)

6. Why don't you double the final consonant in *puff?*
_____

the *k* is preceded by two vowels (*oa*)

7. In adding the suffix *ed* to *soak*, the *k* is not doubled. Why not? _____

the suffix *ly* begins with a consonant (*l*)

8. Even though *dim* ends in a single consonant preceded by a single vowel, you do not double the *m* before *ly*. Why not? _____

a. cupful
b. stopper
c. shrouded
d. mopped
e. witty
f. taxing
g. primly
h. pouter
i. tags
j. deepest
k. pithy
l. kindness

9. Test your skill by adding the suffixes to these one-syllable words.

a. cup   ful   _____

b. stop   er   _____

c. shroud   ed   *shrouded*

d. mop   ed   *mopped*

e. wit   y   *witty*

f. tax   ing   _____

g. prim   ly   _____

h. pout   er   _____

i. tag   s   _____

j. deep   est   _____

k. pith   y   _____

l. kind   ness   _____

10. Words of more than one syllable must also have a single consonant preceded by a single vowel to be doubled. Also, the stress (or accent) must be on the *last* syllable. Take the word *compel.* It ends in *l* preceded by *e*, and the stress is on the last syllable. Because it meets all the requirements, the *l* is doubled before a suffix beginning with a vowel: *compel* + *ed* = *compelled.*

If a word does not meet these requirements, then the final consonant is not doubled. Take the verbs *instill* and *exploit.* Although the accent is on the last syllable in each, the *l* is preceded by another *l* and the *t* is preceded by two vowels. The final consonant *x* is the exception here as well, as the *x* (pronounced like *ks*) counts as two con-

a. d. f.

. . . .

a. 4
b. 1
c. 2
d. 2
e. 1
f. 4
g. 3

sonants. Even though the word *relax* meets the requirements, the x is not doubled.

Now identify those words that have the stress on the last syllable:

a. recur | d. prefer

b. offer | e. enter

c. differ | f. propel

. . . .

Look at and pronounce each word, then match it with the correct explanation for doubling or not doubling.

a. enchant _____ e. compel _____

b. occur _____ f. repeal _____

c. benefit _____ g. determine _____

d. enlighten _____

1. doubles: accent and ending correct
2. does not double: ending correct, but accent is wrong
3. does not double: accent and ending are wrong
4. does not double: accent correct but ending is wrong

a. referred
b. visitor
c. benefited
d. repellent
e. rebuttal
f. repealing
g. occurrence
h. gossipy

11. Applying the doubling rule when appropriate, add the specified suffixes to the following words.

a. refer ed _____

b. visit or _____

c. benefit ed _____

d. repel ent _____

e. rebut al _____

f. repeal ing _____

g. occur ence *occurrence* _____

h. gossip y *gossipy gossipy*

a. c.

12. *Equip* ends in a single consonant preceded by two vowels *u* and *i*. However, only the *i* counts as a vowel because a *u* combined with a *q* makes a *kw* sound (e kwip). *Equip* then meets the requirements of this rule.

There is one suffix before which you do *not* double the p: age.

Choose the suffixes before which you would double the *p* in *equip*.

a. *ing* | c. *ed*

b. *ment* | d. *age*

equipped   equipage
equipment
equipping

13. Add the following suffixes to equip:

ed _____   age _____

ment _____   ing _____

---

transferring
transferred

14. Modern usage permits two pronunciations of *transfer:* tran$\acute{s}$fer or transfe$\acute{r}$. In spelling the word, however, you follow the doubling rule. Add *ing* and *ed* to this word.

_____   _____

---

a. controlling
b. occurred
c. equipped
d. difference
e. beginning
f. transferred
g. happened
h. revealed
i. appearance
j. benefited
k. recurring
l. patrolling
m. relaxing

15. Now combine the root word and suffix for each sentence.

a. The nurse had a difficult time _____ the
control *ing*
patient.

b. This same situation has _____ many times.
occur *ed*

c. The kitchen was _____ with the latest appliances.
equip *ed*

d. Many cannot see the _____ between the two
differ *ence*
items.

e. Since I lost my place, I will have to start reading from the _____.
begin *ing*

f. My father has been _____ to Detroit.
transfer *ed*

g. What has _____ to the Olsons?
happen *ed*

h. A thorough study of the project _____ several
reveal *ed*
statistical errors.

i. The prima donna has made only one concert _____ this year.
appear *ance*

j. Many peasants have _____ from the agrarian
benefit *ed*
reform program.

k. The invalid was plagued by a _____ fever.
recur *ing*

l. The municipal police department does a good job of _____ the area.
patrol *ing*

m. Fishing can be a _____ sport.
relax *ing*

The *l* was doubled before the suffix, so the extra *l* must be taken off to form the original word

a. control
b. excel
c. repel
d. compel

chagrined

chagrin

chagrined

last
first
second *r*

yes

excellent excellence

no

double

16. Sometimes the word that requires doubling is misspelled. Take *rebellion*, for example. The word is made up of two parts, the root and the suffix. Take away the suffix *ion* and you have "rebell." This is the wrong spelling of the root. Why? _____

17. Now reduce these words to their roots.

a. controlled _____

b. excellent _____

c. repelling _____

d. compeller _____

18. The word *chagrin*, which means mental distress, ends in a single consonant preceded by a single vowel and the stress is on the last syllable. But it is an exception to the doubling rule. Add the suffix *ed* to this word. _____

19. The word which means mental distress is an exception to the doubling rule. That word is _____.

20. If a person is suffering from embarrassment or distress caused by failure he is _____.

21. If the addition of a suffix causes the stress to be shifted to an earlier syllable, then the final consonant is not doubled. Let us add *ed* and then *ence* to occur: *occurred* and *occurrence*. There has been no shift in accent as it is still on occúr. Now add *ed* and *ence* to *refer*. On what syllable is the stress in *referred* (first, last)? _____ in *reference* (first, last)? _____ What letter is missing in the second word? _____

22. In your mind add *ence* to these words: *prefer, confer, infer, defer*. Are these examples of words in which the accent shifts to an earlier syllable? _____

23. Now pronounce these words: *excelled excelling excellent excellence*. The root word is *excel*, which has the stress on the last syllable. In which of the above words, if any, does the accent shift? _____

24. Do *excellent* and *excellence* follow the same spelling pattern as *reference*? _____

25. *Excel* is then an exception. Regardless of the shift in stress to an earlier syllable, you still _____ the final *l*.

excel

26. What is the root of *excellent* or *excelling?* _____

a. conference
b. referred
c. excellent
d. preference
e. conferred
f. deferring
g. reference
h. excelled

27. Pronounce the following complete words carefully. Then write them.

a. confer   *ence*   _____

b. refer   *ed*   _____

c. excel   *ent*   _____

d. prefer   *ence*   _____

e. confer   *ed*   _____

f. defer   *ing*   *deferring*

g. refer   *ence*   *reference*

h. excel   *ed*   *excelled*

yes
yes
no

28. The last few words to be studied also end in a single consonant preceded by a single vowel (*ic*). But the stress is not on the last syllable, so the final *c* is not doubled. There is a pronunciation problem, however, and these words must be treated for it. Take the word *picnic*. The final *c* has a hard sound (as in *cat*), not a soft sound (as in *city*), and to preserve this hard sound you must add a *k* before a suffix beginning with a vowel (or the suffix *y*). You do *not* need the *k* if the suffix begins with a consonant, like *ry* or *some*.
Pronounce these words: *traffic panic colic mimic*
Does the final *c* have a hard sound? _____
Is the *k* necessary before a vowel suffix? _____
Is the *k* necessary before a consonant suffix? _____

a. panicked
b. trafficker
c. frolicsome
d. colicky
e. mimicry
f. mimicking

29. Add the specified suffixes to these "ic" words.

a. panic   *ed*   _____   d. colic   *y*   _____

b. traffic   *er*   _____   e. mimic   *ry*   _____

c. frolic   *some*   _____   f. mimic   *ing*   _____

REVIEW

a. e. g. h.

30. In general, what factors must be present to double the final consonant of a word having more than one syllable?

a. the suffix begins with a vowel (or is the suffix *y*)

b. the suffix begins with a consonant

c. the final consonant is preceded by one or more vowels

d. the final consonant is preceded by one or more consonants

e. the final consonant is preceded by a single vowel

f. the accent can be on any syllable

g. the accent is on the last syllable

h. the consonant *x* is not doubled

a. shifts
b. excel
c. chagrin

31. The exceptions to this rule are
a. you do not double if the accent _____ back to an earlier syllable
b. one word doubles regardless of a shift in stress—it is

_____

c. the word meaning mental distress does not double—it is _____

a. occurrence
b. difference
c. equipped
d. controlling
e. benefited
f. beginning
g. existence
h. equipment
i. equipage
j. transferred
k. reference
l. preferred
m. excellent
n. relaxed
o. picnicking

32. Now test your skill in adding the specified suffixes to these words, applying the doubling rules when appropriate.

a. occur   ence   *occurrence*

b. differ   ence   *differrence*

c. equip   ed   *equipped*

d. control   ing

e. benefit   ed

f. begin   ing

g. exist   ence

h. equip   ment

i. equip   age

j. transfer   ed

k. refer   ence

l. prefer   ed

m. excel   ent

n. relax   ed

o. picnic   ing

a. propel
b. control
c. rebel
d. excel
e. compel
f. deter

33. Write the root words from these combined forms.

a. propeller _____

b. controlled _____

c. rebellion _____

> d. excelling _____
> e. compelled _____
> f. deterred _____

POSTTEST

Write the complete words.

1. refer   ence   *referrence*
2. allot   er   *allotter*
3. control   ing   *Controllng*
4. gallop   ed   *galloped*
5. prefer   ing   *prefer*
6. excel   ence   *excellence*
7. frolic   some _____
8. begin   ing _____
9. confer   ence _____
10. mimic   ing _____
11. refer   ed _____
12. rebel   ion _____
13. chagrin   ing _____
14. panic   y _____
15. visit   or _____
16. occur   ence _____
17. skim   ing _____
18. mimic   ry _____
19. differ   ence _____
20. equip   ed _____
21. relax   ed _____
22. exist   ence _____
23. transfer   ing _____
24. defer   ence _____
25. conceal   ed _____

Chapter 11

THE FINAL *E*

When adding a suffix do you drop the final e of a word, or do you keep it? That question is answered in this chapter, and by working carefully through the frames you will learn the rules for dropping or retaining the final e and you will apply the rules to a number of useful words. At the same time you will learn to spell them quickly and unhesitatingly and use them in various contexts. Also you will identify the exceptions to the rules and write them correctly in and out of context.

PRETEST

Add the specified suffixes and write the complete words.

1. desire	*ing*	_____	16. rare	*ity*	_____
2. use	*less*	_____	17. singe	*ing*	_____
3. service	*able*	_____	18. manage	*able*	_____
4. due	*ly*	_____	19. argue	*ing*	_____
5. dense	*ity*	_____	20. adventure	*some*	_____
6. advantage	*ous*	_____	21. dine	*er*	_____
7. come	*ing*	_____	22. canoe	*ist*	_____
8. receive	*able*	_____	23. enforce	*able*	_____
9. argue	*ment*	_____	24. whole	*ly*	_____
10. write	*ing*	_____	25. indispense	*able*	_____
11. true	*ly*	_____	26. nine	*th*	_____
12. change	*able*	_____	~~27. write~~	~~*ing*~~	_____
13. whole	*some*	_____	28. manage	*ment*	_____
14. advertise	*ment*	_____	29. accurate	*ly*	_____
15. lose	*ing*	_____	30. dye	*ing*	_____

a. b. d. e.
· · · · · · · · · · · · ·
b. d. f.
· · · · · · · · · · · · ·
a. c. d.

Coming

Curry

1. When you add a suffix beginning with a *vowel* to a word ending in a silent e you usually drop the e before adding the suffix. Words like *come, write,* or *desire,* end in a silent e—the last sound you hear is the consonant preceding the e: come, write, desire. Words like *thee, devotee,* or *Jeanie,* sound the e so they are not words with the silent e. Notice, too, that the last three end in a double vowel, not a consonant followed by the silent e. Let us look at come and the suffix *ing.* Both meet the requirements of the rule so you would drop the e: *coming.*
Check the words below that end in a silent e.

a. use *using*   d. dine
b. surprise *surprising*   e. relate
c. devotee *devottee*   f. Swanee
· ·
Pick out the suffixes that can require the silent e to be dropped.

a. ly   c. ment   e. some
b. ing *vowel*   d. able   f. ity
· ·
Choose the combinations of words and suffixes to which this rule applies.

a. write   ing   d. advance   ed
b. advise   ment   e. adventure some
c. desire   ous   f. vile   ness

a. dining
b. receivable
c. writing
d. useless
e. desirous
f. advertising
g. rudeness

2. Write the complete words, applying the rule as appropriate.

a. dine   ing   *dining*
b. receive   able   *receivable*
c. write   ing   *writing*
d. use   less   *useless*
e. desire   ous   *desirous*
f. advertise ing   *Advertising*
g. rude   ness   *rudeness*

lose
silent
vowel
drop

3. Now take the word *losing.* It is spelled correctly because
the root word is (*lose, los*) _____
the root ends in a (silent, pronounced) e _____
the suffix begins with a (vowel, consonant) _____
before adding this suffix you (keep, drop) the e_____

a. desire
b. write
c. conceive
d. suppose
e. hope
f. use

4. The words below have also been formed from roots ending in a silent e. So that you will always recognize the parts of such combinations, write the root words.

a. desirous   *desirouse*

b. writing   _____

c. conceivable   _____

d. supposed   _____

e. hoping   _____

f. using   _____

a. accuse   accusing
b. receive   received
c. surprise
   surprising
d. guide   guidance
e. dine   dinette
f. value   valued

5. Now perform two steps: (1) Write the root word from these combinations and then (2) add the specified suffix to it.

	Root	Suffix	Complete word
a. accuser	_____	*ing*	_____
b. receivable	_____	*ed*	_____
c. surprised	_____	*ing*	_____
d. guiding	_____	*ance*	_____
e. dining	_____	*ette*	_____
f. valuable	_____	*ed*	_____

writing

a. writing
b. coming
c. dining
d. pleasurable
e. receivable
f. dividing
g. receiving
h. using
i. density
j. argued
k. indispensable

coming

dining

pleasurable

6. Combine the word and suffixes and write the complete word for each sentence.

a. My cousin is _____ a novel.
   write   *ing*

b. Do you know if Marty is _____?
   come   *ing*

c. When we walked into the cafe we saw Miss Nash _____ with her niece.
   dine   *ing*

d. Sleigh riding is a _____ winter activity.
   pleasure   *able*

e. The student had difficulty understanding the term "_____ goods."
   receive   *able*

f. Uncle Joe is _____ his money between his
   divide   *ing*
daughter and his niece.

g. For several weeks Mr. Green has been _____ mysterious calls.
   receive   *ing*

h. How many books are you _____?

use   ing

i. We could not see the dome of the Capitol because of the _____ of the fog.

dense   ity

j. Sam and his sister _____ for hours.

argue   ed

k. Logical thinking is _____ to good writing.

indispense   able

soft
drop
keep

7. Some "silent e" words with the soft sound of *g* retain the *ge* before certain suffixes, like *able* and *ous*. Take *change*, for instance. The *g* is soft (as in *gem*), not hard (as in *go*). Before suffixes like *ing*, *er*, or *ed* you follow the rule and drop the e: *changing*, *changer*, *changed*. But before the suffix *able* you must keep the e to preserve the soft sound of *g*: *changeable*.

Pronounce the words *manage* and *advantage*.
Do they have the (hard, ~~soft~~) sound of *g*? _____
Do you (keep, ~~drop~~) the e before *ing* or *ed*? _____
Do you (~~keep~~, drop) the e before *able* or *ous*? _____

a. managing
b. changeable
c. advantageous
d. manageable
e. disadvantaged
f. changer

8. Combine these words and suffixes.

a. manage   ing   *managing*

b. change   able   *changeable*

c. advantage   ous   *Advantageous*

d. manage   able   *manageable*

e. disadvantage   ed   *disadvantaged*

f. change   er   *changer*

soft
drop
keep
· · · · · · · · · · · · ·
a. noticing
b. serviceable
c. enforced
d. servicing
e. noticeable
f. enforceable

9. Some "silent e" words with the soft sound of *c* retain the *ce* before the suffix *able*. The *c* in *notice*, for example, has the soft sound (as in *city*) not the hard sound (as in *cat*). For suffixes like *ing*, *er*, *ed*, you follow the general rule and drop the e, but for the suffix *able* you keep the e: *noticing—noticeable*.

Now pronounce these: *service enforce*
Do they have the (soft, hard) sound of *c*? _____
Do you (drop, keep) the e before *ing* or *er*? _____
Do you (keep, drop) the e before *able*? _____

· ·

Combine the words and suffixes below.

a. notice   ing   *Noticing*

b. service   able   *Serviceable*

c. enforce   *ed*   _____

d. service   *ing*   _____

e. notice   *able*   _____

f. enforce   *able*   _____

c.   d.

10. Pick out the suffixes that require the e after a soft c or *g* to be kept.

a. *ed*   b. *ing*   c. *able*   d. *ous*   f. *er*

a. advantageous
b. noticing
   changeable
c. manageable
   managing
d. enforceable
e. disadvantaged
f. pronounceable

11. Write the complete word for each.

a. The proposal is _____ to both factions.
                            advantage *ous*

b. I kept _____ John's _____
              notice *ing*   change *able*
attitude.

c. Although her child is not _____ Mrs. Brown
                              manage *able*
is _____ to put up with the temper tantrums.
     manage *ing*

d. That law is not _____.
                    enforce *able*

e. The minority members will be _____ by
                                 disadvantage *ed*
the new rules.

f. The words are not _____.
                   pronounce *able*

c.   e.
a.   b.   d.   f.

12. You have been adding suffixes beginning with a vowel to words ending in a silent e. Now let us turn to suffixes beginning with a consonant. Generally, the e is retained before such endings. The word *use* is a good example. Before *ing, er,* and *ed* you drop the e: *using, user, used.* But before *ful* you keep the e: *useful.* Here is a list of suffixes:

a. *ness*   c. *ing*   e. *able*
b. *s*   d. *ly*   f. *ment*

Before which suffixes will you drop the e? _____
Before which will you keep the e? _____

a. using
b. user
c. useless
d. uses
e. useful
f. used
g. usage

13. Now add these suffixes to the root word *use.*

a. *ing*   _____   e. *ful*   _____

b. *er*   _____   f. *ed*   _____

c. *less*   _____   g. *age*   _____

d. *s*   _____

a. advertises
b. advertising
c. advertisement
d. advertiser

14. Using *advertise* as the root, add these suffixes to it.

a. *s* _____   c. *ment* _____

b. *ing* _____   d. *er* _____

a. arrangement
b. sincerely
   sincerity
c. accurately
d. ninety

15. Write the complete word(s) for each sentence.

a. What kind of _____ does Sue have for
                     arrange   ment
babysitting?

b. Although Tom acts _____ toward his sister,
                          sincere *ly*
his _____ can sometimes be questioned.
      sincere *ity*

c. The students computed every example _____.
                                          accurate *ly*

d. In our college over _____ percent of the profes-
                          nine *ty*
sors are fifty years or older.

ninety
ninth

16. In the preceding frame you simply added *ty* to *nine*
because the *ty* begins with a consonant. Adding *th* to
nine, however, constitutes an exception. So nine + ty =
_____, but nine + th = _____.

ninety
ninth

17. Out of a class of one hundred and _____, Henry
                                            nine *ty*
Bowen was _____ from the top.
              nine *th*

drop

18. Another exception is the combination of *argue* and
ment. Even though *ment* begins with a consonant, it is
treated like a suffix beginning with a vowel. So you would
(drop, keep) the e in *argue*. _____

a. argument
b. argued
c. arguing
d. arguable

19. Add these suxffixes to *argue*.

a. *ment* _____   c. *ing* _____

b. *ed* _____   d. *able* _____

arguing
argument

20. Although the different factions have been _____
                                                   argue *ing*
for an hour, the _____ has not been an emo-
                    argue *ment*
tional exchange of words.

REVIEW

a. ninth
b. advertisements
c. coming
d. receiving
e. useful
f. choosing
g. writing
h. scarcity
i. immensity
j. argument
k. ninety
l. useless
m. management

21. Test your skill by writing the complete word(s) for each sentence.

a. Nancy was the _____ entry in the beauty con-
nine th

test.

b. Some _____ can mislead the reader.
advertise ments

c. Are you _____ to the diner soon?
come ing

d. Are you still _____ seed catalogs?
receive ing

e. There are several _____ remedies on the market.
use ful

f. What color hat will you be _____?
choose ing

g. An art that is not easy to master is the art of _____.
write ing

h. The heavy rains caused a _____ of berries.
scarce ity

i. The farmer was impressed by the _____ of
immense ity
the canning factory.

j. Who will lose the _____?
argue ment

k. There were _____ entries.
nine ty

l. To talk any more about the merger is _____.
use less

m. There is friction between employees and _____.
manage ment

a. canoed
b. hoes
c. shoer
d. canoeing
e. hoer
f. shoeing
g. canoeist
h. shoes

22. Words ending in *oe*, like *canoe*, also follow the general rules for keeping the e before a suffix beginning with a consonant or dropping the e before a suffix beginning with a vowel. The one exception is a suffix beginning with *i*—here you must keep the e.
Add the specified suffixes.

a. canoe   *ed*   _____

b. hoe   *s*   _____

c. shoe   *er*   _____

d. canoe   *ing*   _____

e. hoe   er   _____

f. shoe   ing   _____

g. canoe   ist   _____

h. shoe   s   _____

shoeing

23. Ted is spending his summer _____ his uncle's

shoe *ing*

horses.

24. Although Joan _____ for five hours yesterday,

canoe *ed*

canoed
canoeing
canoeist

she will go _____ tomorrow because she wants to

canoe *ing*

become an expert _____.

canoe *ist*

hoed

25. I've never _____ so much in my life.

hoe *ed*

a. dying
   dyeing
b. singing
   singeing

26. To avoid confusion, the silent e at the end of two words, *singe* and *dye*, must be retained before *ing*. *Singeing* means scorching or burning; *dyeing* means coloring. If you drop the e before the *ing* you will write two different words: *singing* and *dying*. Choose the appropriate words for each sentence below.

a. Although Mary's mother was slowly _____ from cancer, she spent an hour yesterday _____ Mary's coat.

b. **The cooks concentrated so much on their _____ that they didn't do a good job of _____ the hair from the chickens.**

a. dyed
b. singes
c. dyer
d. singeing
e. dyes
f. dyeing
g. singed

27. If the suffix *ing* is the only exception for the words *singe* and *dye*, you follow the general rules for either dropping or keeping the final e. Add the specified suffixes to these two words.

a. dye   ed   _____

b. singe   s   _____

c. dye   er   _____

d. singe   ing   _____

e. dye   s   _____

f. dye   ing   _____

g. singe   ed   _____

drop
duly
truly
wholly

28. The last three words to be studied *due, true, whole,* follow the general rule for the silent e before a suffix beginning with a consonant except for *ly*. So before *ly* you would (drop, keep) the e in these words. _____ Now add *ly* and write the complete words. _____

_____ _____

a. truly
b. dues
c. wholesome
d. trues
e. duly
f. trueness
g. wholly
h. wholeness

29. Write the complete words for all these "silent e" words.

a. true   ly   _____
b. due   s   _____
c. whole   some   _____
d. true   s   _____
e. due   ly   _____
f. true   ness   _____
g. whole   ly   _____
h. whole   ness   _____

due
true
whole

30. Name the three words that drop the final e before *ly*.

_____ _____ _____

REVIEW

a. wholly
b. hoeing
canoeing

31. Add the words and suffixes and write the complete words.

a. His actions were *wholely* unforgivable.
whole ly

b. While some teenagers spent the afternoon *hoeing*
hoe ing

c. dyeing
d. truly
e. singeing
f. shoed
g. duly
h. wholesome

_____, others went *canoeing*.
canoe ing

c. The process of putting coloring permanently into fibers of cotton or wool is called *dyeing*.
dye ing

d. I am *truly* sorry for my rudeness.
true ly

e. Becky keeps *singeing* her hair with the
singe ing

hot curling iron.

f. The blacksmith *shoed* all the horses yesterday.
shoe ed

g. The newly elected commissioner will begin his reform program within a *duely* specified time.
due ly

h. Her two nephews are *wholesome* youngsters.
whole some

2⟌184 92
180
4

POSTTEST

Add the specified suffix to each word and write the complete word.

1. achieve	ment	*Achiev*		16. hope	less		
2. advise	able	_____		17. receive	ing		
3. canoe	ing	_____		18. dense	ity		
4. pleasure	able	_____		19. pursue	er		
5. manage	able	_____		20. whole	ly		
6. age	less	_____		21. change	able		
7. canoe	ist	_____		22. ache	ing		
8. notice	able	_____		23. desire	ous		
9. judge	ing	_____		24. advantage	ous		
10. remote	ness	_____		25. rare	ity		
11. true	ly	_____		26. achieve	ing		
12. true	ness	_____		27. imagine	able		
13. singe	ing	_____		28. hoe	ing		
14. disadvantage	ed	_____		29. argue	ment		
15. argue	ing	_____		30. pronounce	able		

Handwritten notes:

Continuity

Achievment
Advisable
Canoeing
pleasureable

pursuing
judgment
continuity
deciveness
desiciveness
Acknowledg
Acknowledgment

Abridgment
Continuity
Rehearsal
Rehearsal
RE HEAR sal

decisiveness
Awful
prestigious
adherence
awful

Chapter 12

THE FINAL Y

Have you had words like *studying*, *angrily*, or *tries* underscored and marked with "sp" in the margin? Even if this has only happened occasionally, this chapter will be worthwhile for you to read, because by the end of it you will know when to keep the *y* or when to change it to *i* before a suffix. By learning and applying the rules and spelling a number of common and useful "final y" words, both in and out of context, you will master the techniques needed to distinguish between those words that follow the rules and those that do not, and to recognize the exceptions immediately. In the case of plurals of words ending in *y*, you will spell them accurately as well as reduce them to their singular form, ensuring the spelling of both forms correctly at all times.

PRETEST

Combine the root and suffix and write the complete word.

1.	accompany	*ment*	accompaniment	11.	apply	*ing*	applying
2.	convey	*s*	conveys	12.	happy	*ly*	happily
3.	occupy	*ing*	occupying	13.	carry	*ing*	carrying
4.	copy	*ist*	copyist	14.	hungry	*ly*	hungrily
5.	story	*es*	stories	15.	beauty	*ful*	beautiful
6.	bury	*al*	burial	16.	dormitory	*es*	dormitories
7.	beauty	*es*	beauties	17.	happy	*ness*	happiness
8.	employ	*er*	employer	18.	day	*ly*	daily
9.	try	*es*	tries	19.	study	*ing*	studying
10.	tragedy	*es*	tragedies	20.	pity	*ful*	pitiful

21. display	*ing*	*displaying*	
22. company	*es*	*Companies*	
23. pity	*ing*	*pitying*	
24. cozy	*ly*	*Cozily*	
25. chimney	*s*	*Chimneys*	

26. society	*es*	*Societies*	
27. try	*al*	*Trial*	
28. theory	*es*	*Theories*	
29. accompany	*ed*	*accompanied*	
30. industry	*es*	*industries*	

a. d. e.
· · · · · · · · · · · · ·
b. relaying
c. surveys
e. displayed
g. destroyer
h. alleys

1. Here is the general rule: when a final *y* is preceded by a *vowel*, you keep the *y* before adding a suffix. Take *journey*, which ends in *y* preceded by the vowel *e*. If you add *s* to form the plural, or *ed* or *ing* to make verb forms, you keep the *y*: *journeys, journeyed, journeying.* How about the noun *penny?* or *party?* Both end in *y* but both are preceded by a consonant. So these words do not meet the requirements of the rule.

From the list below identify those words to which this final *y* rule applies.

a. relay	*relaying*	d. destroy	_____
b. pity	*pity.*	e. monkey	_____
c. hungry	_____	f. clumsy	_____

· ·

Now pick out only those words to which the rule applies, add the specified suffixes, and write the complete words.

a. beauty	*es*	*beauties*
b. relay	*ing*	*relaying*
c. survey	*s*	*surveys*
d. baby	*es*	*babies*
e. display	*ed*	*displayed*
f. duty	*es*	*duties*
g. destroy	*er*	*destroyer*
h. alley	*s*	*alleys*

a. medleys
b. trolleys
c. pulleys
d. destroyed
e. portrayal
f. surveying
g. chimneys

2. Write the complete word for each sentence.

a. The symphony played several *medleys* in last
　　　　　　　　　　　　　　　medley s
night's concert.

b. Electric cars can also be called _____.
　　　　　　　　　　　　　　　　　trolley s

c. The heavy concrete blocks were lifted to the top of the tower by _____.
　　　　　　　　pulley s

d. During the air raids in England, many buildings were

_____.

       destroy *ed*

e. I was amused by his _____ of the school-

       portray *al*

teacher.

f. Mike Jones earns his living by _____ the land

       survey *ing*

for highway construction.

g. Black smoke billowed from the two _____.

       chimney *s*

vowel
keep

3. The rule illustrated by the words and suffixes you added above can be stated as: When adding a suffix to a word ending in final *y* preceded by a (vowel, consonant), you (keep, drop) the *y* and add the suffix.

REVIEW

a. enjoyable
b. employment
d. conveyed
e. delaying
g. buyers

4. Combine the words and suffixes below to which this final *y* rule applies. Leave blank any combination that does not follow the rule.

a. Her trip to Peru was _____.

       enjoy *able*

b. I will look for different _____.

       employ *ment*

c. Researchers have found a new feeding formula for

_____.

       baby *es*

d. Her message to the board was _____ yesterday.

       convey *ed*

e. There is no use _____ any longer.

       delay *ing*

f. The information was not _____.

       rely *able*

g. How many fashion _____ does the store have?

       buy *ers*

5. Whereas the final *y* preceded by a vowel is usually retained before a suffix, the final *y* preceded by a consonant is changed to *i* before suffixes that do *not* begin with *i*. For those that begin with *i* you keep the *y*. For example, to form the plural of *copy*, you change the *y* to *i* and add *es*:

copies. Using *copy* as the root word, let us add these suffixes:

copy + er = copier
copy + ed = copied

but

copy + ist = copyist
copy + ing = copying

Check the words below that have the final *y* preceded by a consonant:

a. cemetery _____
b. pulley _____
c. story _____
d. county _____

e. survey _____
f. tragedy _____
g. dictionary _____

Check before which suffixes listed below the final *y* preceded by a consonant is changed to *i*.

a. er _____
b. ing _____
c. ly _____

d. ness _____
e. s _____
f. ist _____

The suffixes that require the final *y* preceded by a consonant to keep the *y* begin with what letter? __i__

From the list below identify which combinations require the *y* to be changed to *i*.

a. mercy ful _____
b. steady ly _____
c. copy ing _____
d. bury al _____

e. study ing _____
f. pity es _____
g. lobby ist _____

6. Now add the suffixes to these "final y" words.

a. vary   ing   *varying* _____

b. accompany   es _____

c. enemy   es _____

d. rely   ance _____

e. pity   ing _____

f. cemetery   es _____

g. angry   ly _____

h. society   es _____

i. wealthy   er _____

j. clumsy   ly _____

k. penny   es _____

l. study   ing _____

a. denied
b. occupying
c. beautiful
d. relies
e. carrying
f. heartily
g. studying

7. Now write the complete words for these sentences.

a. The captured enemy tried to establish his innocence when he _____ any responsibility for the raid.
deny ed

b. This summer the study of plane geometry is _____
occupy ing
most of Andy's time.

c. The reigning queen is _____.
beauty ful

d. The manager _____ too much on the employees.
rely es

e. Yesterday John carried two heavy trunks to the attic, but today he is _____ small cartons up there.
carry ing

f. After a good night's sleep, Mary ate _____.
hearty ly

g. Nora has been _____ too hard.
study ing

days
daily

8. The rule for final y preceded by a vowel applies to the word *day*, except for the suffix *ly*.
Combine *day* and the plural suffix *s*. _____
Now combine *day* and *ly*. _____

a. said
b. laid

9. Like *day*, the words *lay* and *say* generally follow the rule. When you add the past tense ending *ed*, however, you must change the y to i and drop the e in *ed*.
Complete these sentences:

a. I *say* something today, but I _____ it yesterday.

b. Today I lay the book on the chest; yesterday I _____ it there.

b.

10. For the past tense ending *ed*, the word *pay* is treated like *lay* and *say*. But there are two meanings to *pay*. If it means to coat or cover (a ship, for example) with tar or asphalt, you have a choice of spelling: *paid* or *payed*. If *pay* means to compensate, to give money in exchange, then you always write *paid*.
Which sentence below does not allow for an alternate spelling:

a. Twenty workmen _____ the seams of the U.S.S. Harrington in five days.

b. John _____ a hundred dollars for his recorder.

paid or payed

a. saying
b. payed or paid
c. layer
d. said
e. days
f. paid
g. laid

11. What are the spellings allowed for sentence a. in the preceding frame? _____

12. Now add the suffixes to these.

a. say   *ing*   _____   e. day   s   _____
b. pay   *ed*   _____   f. pay   *ed*   _____
   (to coat)   (to recompense)
c. lay   *er*   _____   g. lay   *ed*   _____
d. say   *ed*   _____

a. laid
b. said
c. daily
d. payed or paid
e. laying
f. payable
g. payer paid
payee

13. Combine these words and suffixes.

a. The grandmother _____ the child in her crib.
   lay ed

b. How many times have you _____ it?
   say ed

c. The railroad has a _____ run to Kensington.
   day ly

d. The men stopped working for the day when they _____ the seams.
   pay ed

e. John is _____ new tile.
   lay ing

f. The loan is _____ on the first of each month.
   pay able

g. The person who pays the money is the _____;
   pay er
   the person to whom the money is _____ is the _____.
   pay ed   pay ee

day
society

14. To avoid misspelling some root words, let us reverse the procedure of adding elements. With suffixes being added to a word ending in final *y* preceded by a vowel you simply add the suffix, so in subtracting the suffix you just take it off: *toys* − *s* = *toy*. For a word ending in *y* preceded by a consonant you change the *y* to *i* and add the suffix, so in subtracting the suffix you take off the suffix and replace the *i* with the *y*: *relies* − *es* − *i* + *y* = *rely*.
What is the singular form of *days*? _____
What is the singular form of *societies*? _____

company

15. The word *companies* means several establishments. Just one establishment would be a _____.

lobbies
lobby

16. The hotel has several _____. Just one
   lobby es
would be a _____.

REVIEW

a. denial
b. pities
c. lobbying
d. steadier
e. tragedies
f. cozily
g. cemeteries
h. copyist
i. tries
j. accompanied

17. Test your skill by writing the complete word for each blank.

a. deny	al	_____		f. cozy	ly	_____
b. pity	es	_____		g. cemetery	es	_____
c. lobby	ing	_____		h. copy	ist	_____
d. steady	er	_____		i. try	es	_____
e. tragedy	es	_____		j. accompany	ed	_____

change the y to i
keep

18. Let us restate this rule for the final y preceded by a consonant: before adding a suffix that does not begin with i, you (keep the y, change the y to i). _____
Before a suffix like ist, you (drop, keep) the y. _____

kept

19. Generally, the final y preceded by a vowel is (kept, dropped) before the suffix. _____

a. denial denies
   denied denying
b. portrayal
   portraying
   portrayed
   portrays

20. Now apply the rules to these.

a. deny
   al _____
   es _____
   ed _____
   ing _____

b. portray
   al _____
   ing _____
   ed _____
   s   _____

paid

21. How do you spell the past tense of *pay*, meaning to exchange money? _____

POSTTEST

Combine the roots and suffixes and write the complete words.

1. summary   es   _____
2. annoy   ance _____
3. copy   er   _____
4. rely   es   _____
5. portray   s   _____
6. defy   ing   _____
7. bury   al   _____
8. day   ly   _____

9. pay   ed   _____
   (to recompense)
10. monkey   s   _____
11. society   es   _____
12. employ   ed   _____
13. lobby   ing   _____
14. medley   s   _____
15. cemetery   es   _____

16. tendency   *es*   _____

17. accompany   *ment*   _____

18. key   *ed*   _____

19. try   *ing*   _____

20. lay   *ed*   _____

21. copy   *ist*   _____

22. university   *es*   _____

23. controversy   *es*   _____

24. pity   *less*   _____

25. ready   *ing*   _____

26. deny   *al*   _____

27. luxury   *es*   _____

28. employ   *ment*   _____

29. say   *ed*   _____

30. academy   *es*   _____

Chapter 13

IE OR EI

If you have been plagued by the *ie* and *ei* combinations, wondering when to use one or the other, you need not worry any longer. This chapter will present definite rules for the *ie* and *ei* combinations as well as some exceptions to these rules. In the chapter you will (1) identify the various vowel sounds represented by *ie* or *ei*; (2) apply the rules for combining the e and i; (3) recognize and spell correctly the exceptions; and (4) practice spelling a number of useful "ei-ie" words in and out of context. The chapter will also give you a basis for spelling other familiar or unfamiliar "i" and "e" words.

PRETEST

Fill in the correct combination: *ie* or *ei*.

1. To ease means to rel_____ve.
2. Vanity is another name for conc_____t.
3. To get is to rec_____ve.
4. Two young boys were credited with the s_____zure of the bank robber.
5. To be lacking in something is to be defic_____nt.
6. The postman w_____ghed my packages.
7. The head of a tribe is usually called a ch_____f.
8. Please give me a p_____ce of cake.
9. Strange is a synonym for w_____rd.
10. Another word for forgery is counterf_____t.
11. What is your h_____ght and w_____ght?
12. To accomplish means to ach_____ve.
13. I expect to join the for_____gn service.
14. We live in a blighted n_____ghborhood.
15. How much l_____sure time do you want?

Yes
· · · · · · · · · · · · · ·
d.

1. One of the best ways to select the correct combinations of *i* and *e* is by their sound, as the vowel sound represented by these two letters will usually provide the clue to the correct spelling of a word.

Look at these words carefully, then say them aloud, stressing the underlined part.

piece	niece	siege
chief	deceive	relief
receive	yield	conceit

Check whether the vowel sound of the *i* and *e* is the same for all the words.

Yes _____ No _____

· ·

The vowel sound matches which sound in the underlined portions of the words below? _____

a. bed   b. bay   c. bite   d. beef

no   yes

2. The vowel sound in *beef* is the same as the speech sound represented by the letter *e*—this we call the long e sound. Each word in the list you just pronounced has this long e sound. But the spelling of the *i* and *e* is not the same. Look again at the words:

piece	receive
chief	deceive
niece	conceit
siege	
relief	

The first list has the *ie* and the second *ei*. In the first is the consonant preceding *ie* always the same? _____ Is it in the second? _____ .

ie
ei

3. The consonant then provides the clue. If the consonant is *not* c, you write which combination (*ie, ei*)? _____
If the consonant is *c*, you write it like this: _____ .

a. *ie*
b. *ei*
c. *ie*
d. *ie*
e. *ei*
f. *ie*
g. *ei*

4. Each word below has the long e sound. Write in the correct combination: *ie* or *ei*.

a. y_____ld   e. conc_____t

b. rec_____pt   f. bel_____ved

c. s_____ge   g. rec_____ving

d. ch_____f

a. *ei*
b. *ie*
c. *ie*
d. *ie*
e. *ei*
f. *ie*
g. *ei*

5. Complete the words in these sentences with *ie* or *ei*.

a. She has no cause to dec____ve.

b. Betsy has only one n____ce.

c. The army ended its long s____ge.

d. His statement is hard for me to bel____ve.

e. My aunt has many cash rec____pts.

f. Please give me a p____ce of paper.

g. Lou is more conc____ted than Ted.

a. receive
b. siege
c. achieve
d. relieve
e. deceive

6. At the left is a panel of words requiring *ie* or *ei*. Read each sentence carefully for its meaning, choose the word from the panel, and write the complete word.

dec____ve   a. The principal said I would _____
s____ge   a prize.
ach____ve   b. The fortress withstood the _____
rec____ve   for a full month.
rel____ve   c. I worry that I may not _____
                                                   accomplish

my goal.
d. Many new drugs help to _____
discomfort.
e. Someone who will mislead another will
_____ that person.

ie   ei

7. The usual spelling of *i* and *e* with the long *e* sound is _____ except after *c*; then it is _____.

yes
receive
c

8. Now let us take these words. Look at them closely and pronounce them.

weird   seize   either
leisure   seizure   neither

Do they have the same sound as bel*ie*f and receive? ____
Is the combination of *i* and *e* written as in *belief* or *receive?* _____
To best remember them you can link them with those words with the long *e* sound coming after which conso-nant? ____

neither
seizure
leisure
weird

9. You can also associate them in some way. For exam-ple, two have similar sounds: *either* and n_____.
Another two go together: the verb *seize* and its noun s_____ure. Another rhymes with seizure: l_____.
The one that stands alone is w____rd, meaning strange.

a. either
b. neither
c. seize
d. seizure
e. leisure
f. weird

10. Finish spelling the exceptions:

a. One or another is the definition of e_____.

b. Not one or the other is the meaning of n_____.

c. To grasp is to s_____.

d. The act of grasping is s_____.

e. Free time is called l_____.

f. To be strange is to be w_____.

either
neither
seize
seizure
leisure
weird

11. Write the six exceptions to the long e sound of *i* and e.

_____ _____ _____ _____ _____ _____

no

REVIEW

12. Look at this group of words. Are there any *i*'s and e's out of order? _____

conceive	conceit	receipt
achieve	receive	thief
relief	believe	belief

a. *ie*
b. *ei*
c. *ei*
d. *ei*
e. *ei*
f. *ei*
g. *ie*
h. *ei*

13. Supply the missing *ie* or *ei*.

a. Do you bel_____ve his story?

b. N_____ther Ann nor I will go.

c. Strange is the meaning of w_____rd.

d. How much money will he rec_____ve?

e. Mary Jo has too much l_____sure.

f. The three men tried to s_____ze her.

g. I hope to ach_____ve my goals.

h. Joe is terribly conc_____ted.

c.

14. Check which sound in the underlined portion of the following words matches the sound of the *i* and e in the words to the right.

a. bit

b. beef

c. bay

d. bite

neighbor

freight

weigh

c. e. f. h.

15. All the words below have the *ei* combination. Pick out those with the long *a* sound as in bay.

a. either   e. reign
b. weird   f. reindeer
c. weighty   g. seize
d. leisure   h. sleigh

ei

16. Like the six exceptions to the long e sound, the words with the long *a* sound have which combination (*ie, ei*)?
_____

yes—all are
spelled *ei*

17. Does the long *a* rule apply to the underlined words?
_____

a. During the <u>Reign</u> of Terror thousands of people were executed.
b. Joe hopped on a <u>freight</u> car.
c. One controls a horse with <u>reins</u>.
d. My mother is <u>overweight</u>.
e. <u>Reindeer</u> Lake is in Manitoba.

a. long *a*
b. long *e*
c. long *e*
d. long *a*
e. long *e*
f. long *e*
g. long *a*

18. Now indicate which sound each *i* and *e* combination has.

a. weight _____   e. leisure _____

b. weird _____   f. neither _____

c. seizure _____   g. neighbor _____

d. freight _____

b.

19. In the preceding frame, the words having the long e sound
a. follow the rule for long e.
b. are exceptions to this rule.

a. *ei*
b. *ei*
c. *ei*
d. *ei*

20. Read the sentences first, then fill in the missing *i* and *e* combinations.

a. Some women like v____ls on their hats.

b. A pleasurable sport in the winter is a sl____gh ride.

c. A vessel that carries blood back to the heart is a v____n.

d. How much do you w____gh?

ie
ei
ei

21. Generally, the long e sound of *i* and *e* is written _____ except after c when it is written _____; the long sound of a is written _____.

b.

22. Now pronounce the word *height*. The *ei* corresponds to which sound? _____

a. bed .   b. bite   c. beef   d. bit
e. bay

ei

23. Both the long *a* and long *i* sounds are written (*ie* or *ei*)? _____

ei

24. When one measures how tall he is, he measures his h____ght.

height

25. The word meaning tallness is often misspelled not only because of the *ei*, but because of the ending: Johnny is nearly the h____gh__ of his father.

a. ei ei
b. ei
c. ei
d. ei
e. ei

26. Read each sentence first, then write the correct combination(s) of *i* and *e*.

a. What is your w____ght and h____ght?

b. The troops numbered ____ghty thousand.

c. I wonder how long this king will r____gn.

d. After dark Tim sneaked down to hop on a fr____ght.

e. If you want to control your horse, tighten the r____ns.

d.

27. Now look at these words closely and pronounce them:
     foreign   counterfeit
The sound of the *ei* corresponds to which underlined sound below:

a. bay   b. bite   c. beef   d. bit

ei ei

28. The short *i* sound is in the words *counterf____t* and *for____gn*.

feit

29. An imitation or forgery is the definition of the noun *counter____*.

eign

30. To be alien to one's nature is to be *for____* to it.

ei
ei ei

31. The short *i* is also apparent in three other words: *forf____t   surf____t   sover____gn*

feit
feit

32. To surrender a privilege for committing an offense is to *for____*; to feed to excess or to overindulge is to *sur____*.

ei

33. A king or queen can also be called a *sover____gn*.

counterfeit
surfeit
forfeit

foreign
sovereign

34. Three words having the same short *i* sound of *i* and *e* are _____*feit*, _____*feit*, and _____ *feit*.

35. Two words having the same ending with the short *i* sound of *i* and *e* are _____*gn* and _____*gn*.

a. *ei*   short *i*
b. *ei*   long *a*
c. *ei*   long *i*
d. *ei*   short *i*
e. *ei*   long *a*
f. *ei*   short *i*
g. *ei*   long *a*

REVIEW

36. Fill in the missing *i* and *e* combinations for each word and identify the vowel sound of each.

Vowel
sound

Vowel
sound

a. for____gn   _____

e. r____gn   _____

b. w____ghty   _____

f. forf____t   _____

c. h____ght   _____

g. r____ndeer   _____

d. counterf____t   _____

long *a*
long *i*
short *i*

37. The *ei* combination has three vowel sounds: _____ a, _____ *i*, and _____ *i*.

a. *eign*
b. *eigh* *ei*
c. *feit*
d. *eight*
e. *feit*
f. *eigners*

38. Now complete the "ie-ei" words.

a. Nancy accepted a job in the for_____ service.

b. Only five boys w_____ over ____ghty pounds.

c. John must for_____ a day's pay.

d. Mary's h_____ prevents her from playing basketball.

e. Sam was convicted of printing counter_____ money.

f. The U.S. admits a quota of for_____ each year.

shent

39. Now let us take *efficient* and divide it first into syllables: ef   fi   cient. Pronounce them. The last has which sound ("sent," "shent")? _____

the "sh"

40. Because we are interested in the *i* and *e*, what part of the "shent" sound in *cient* does the *cie* have?

cie

41. This "sh" sound then is represented by the letters _____ .

42. Do these adjectives also have the "sh" sound of *cie*?

_____

proficient   sufficient   deficient

yes

43. Let us look at the four words again: *proficient, suffi-cient, deficient, efficient.* Which two syllables are spelled the same? _____

second and third
(*fi   cient*)

44. Only the first syllable differs. To be effective is to be _____ficient; to be enough, or to suffice, is to be _____ficient. The prefix *pro* means forward and *de* means away or down. If one is skilled in a trade (gone forward, in other words) he is said to be _____ficient; if he has gone down or is lacking in some way he is _____ficient.

ef suf
pro
de

45. Write the correct "shent" words for each sentence.

a. There will be _____ food for the
picnic.   enough

b. This is the most _____ way to
operate the machine.   effective

c. Despite their education, they are _____
in their knowledge of the English language.   wanting

d. In his layout work at the printshop he is _____.
skilled

a. sufficient
b. efficient
c. deficient
d. proficient

46. The state of being efficient is *efficiency.* In spelling the noun you drop the _____ from the adjective and add

_____.

t
cy

47. How would you spell these nouns?

a. the state of being enough _____

b. the state of being wanting _____

c. the state of being skilled _____

a. sufficiency
b. deficiency
c. proficiency

REVIEW

48. When *i* and *e* are preceded by *c* and have the "sh" sound, the letters are combined like this: _____.

cie

a. deficient
b. sufficient
c. efficient
d. proficient
e. efficiency

49. Supply the "cie" words to fit each definition.

a. to be wanting _____

b. to be enough _____

c. to be effective _____

d. to be skilled _____

e. the state of being effective _____

POSTTEST

Fill in the correct combination: *ie* or *ei*.

1. I cannot bel____ve your story.

2. The Army finally ended its long s____ge.

3. He thinks he has a sover____gn right to do that.

4. Where is the fr____ght office?

5. I expect to rec____ve four presents.

6. He must forf____t all his privileges.

7. Have you seen any r____ndeer?

8. Sandy Black is very effic____nt.

9. Don't y____ld to the demands.

10. As he comes around the corner, try to s____ze him.

11. How much do you w____gh?

12. To be lacking means to be defic____nt.

13. He has a reputation as a th____f.

14. I am working so hard I have no l____sure time.

15. The child told a w____rd story.

Chapter 14

PLURALS

There are just two plural endings, but not knowing when to use one or the other can present some problems. In this chapter you will learn specific rules for each ending, apply the rules to a number of words and write these plurals in context, recognize the exceptions and spell them correctly. You will also change various plurals back to the singular so that you will not misspell either form.

PRETEST

Write the plurals of the following nouns.

1. display _____
2. penalty _____
3. gas _____
4. veto _____
5. zoo _____
6. monarch _____
7. inquiry _____
8. crisis _____
9. Negro _____
10. melody _____
11. perch _____
12. thief _____
13. potato _____
14. Tommy _____
15. wish _____

16. buzz _____
17. university _____
18. Tory _____
19. discrepancy _____
20. grief _____
21. half _____
22. society _____
23. gulf _____
24. elegy _____
25. datum _____
26. hero _____
27. wife _____
28. study _____
29. decoy _____
30. tax _____

1. Two suffixes are used to form the plural from the singular: s and es. Most words take just s. For instance, the plural of *table* is *tables,* of *book* is *books,* and of *chair* is *chairs.* Certain other words need es to form the plural because just an s would make them difficult or impossible to pronounce. Take *dress* or *gas* that already end in s. Another s would only extend the original "s" sound, not make another syllable that is needed to pronounce the plural: *dress es, gas es.* The same problem applies to words ending in *sh* and *tch.* If you try pronouncing *dish* and *ditch* with just another s (as in *dishs* and *ditchs*) you will hear just an "s" sound after the *sh* or *tch,* not a distinct syllable, as in *dish es* or *ditch es.*

Apply these rules to make the plural forms of the nouns below.

a. princess _____   g. wish _____

b. airship _____   h. screen _____

c. clutch _____   i. pitch _____

d. seedling _____   j. address _____

e. crash _____   k. match _____

f. concert _____

2. Like those words ending in s, *sh*, and *tch*, those ending in x and z, like *tax* and *buzz*, need more than the s to form a pronounceable plural ending. How would you write the plurals of tax and buzz? _____ _____

3. The plural ending for a word ending in *ch* depends on the sound of the *ch*. If it has the soft sound (as in *church*) you add es. If it has the hard sound (as in *epoch*) you add s.

Indicate by S (soft) or H (hard) which sound of *ch* these words have.

a. arch _____   d. peach _____

b. lurch _____   e. epoch _____

c. monarch _____   f. porch _____

· ·

Now add the correct plural endings to the above words.

_____   _____   _____

_____   _____   _____

4. Now we have another general rule for forming plurals. Using this list as a guide, write the consonant endings that require es: _____

dress   bush   porch   match   fox   waltz

es

5. Words ending in s, sh, ch (soft), x, and z take _____ to form the plural.

a. matches
b. transplants
c. bungalows
d. dishes
e. monarchs
f. organs
g. taxes
h. splashes
i. stairs
j. compresses
k. bookcases
l. pitches
m. waltzes
n. lurches

6. Apply the rules presented thus far and form the plurals.

a. match _____ h. splash _____
b. transplant _____ i. stair _____
c. bungalow _____ j. compress _____
d. dish _____ k. bookcase _____
e. monarch _____ l. pitch _____
f. organ _____ m. waltz _____
g. tax _____ n. lurch _____

a. s
b. es
c. s
d. es
e. es
f. s
g. s
h. es
i. es
j. s
k. es
l. s

7. Nouns ending in y preceded by a vowel usually take s to form the plural. For example, *attorney* ends in y preceded by e, so its plural is *attorneys*. On the other hand, most nouns ending in y preceded by a consonant take es and the y is changed to i before the es. *Party* ends in y preceded by t, so its plural is *parties*.
From the list below decide which words take s and which take es.

a. decoy _____ g. pulley _____
b. lullaby _____ h. dormitory _____
c. tray _____ i. tragedy _____
d. clergy _____ j. display _____
e. melody _____ k. duty _____
f. bay _____ l. attorney _____

a. studies
b. ploys
c. days
d. elegies
e. dailies
f. replies
g. buoys
h. inquiries
i. frays
j. cemeteries
k. trolleys
l. joys

8. Now write the plurals for these singular nouns.

a. study _____ g. buoy _____
b. ploy _____ h. inquiry _____
c. day _____ i. fray _____
d. elegy _____ j. cemetery _____
e. daily _____ k. trolley _____
f. reply _____ l. joy _____

a. Bettys Tonys
b. Kellys

9. Proper names (first and last) ending in *y* preceded by either a vowel or consonant take *s* so that the name will not be changed. For instance, the Kennedy family can be called the Kennedys. More than one Libby would be Libbys and more than one boy named Harry would be Harrys. Some proper nouns, however, take *es* because they are not names of specific individuals. The plural of *Tory* (a member of a British political party in the seventeenth century) would be *Tories*. Note that the *y* is changed to *i* before adding *es*.

a. If you write about several girls named Betty and several boys named Tony, how would you write the plurals?

_____ _____

b. All the members of the Kelly family would be called the _____.

a. deputies
b. Anthonys
c. properties
d. Crosbys
e. Tories
f. societies

10. Write the correct plurals for these words.

a. deputy _____   d. Crosby _____

b. Anthony _____   e. Tory _____

c. property _____   f. society _____

a. drays
b. Sibleys
c. countries
d. envoys
e. Henrys
f. plays
g. treaties
h. counties

11. Now apply all the rules about plurals you have learned thus far and write the correct forms for these words ending in *y*.

a. dray _____   e. Henry _____

b. Sibley _____   f. play _____

c. country _____   g. treaty _____

d. envoy _____   h. county _____

a. d. e. f.
b. c.

12. Sometimes the singular form is incorrectly formed from the plural. So that you do not make this mistake, let us practice forming the singular. As you remember, you form the plural of words ending in *y* preceded by a vowel by adding *s*. The singular is formed by subtracting the *s*. For words ending in *y* preceded by a consonant you must subtract *es* and change the *i* back to the original *y*.
Which of the following would end in *y* preceded by a consonant in the singular? _____

a. discrepancies   d. bullies

b. holidays   e. cemeteries

c. chimneys   f. lobbies

To form the singular which ones would have the *s* subtracted? _____

a. discrepancy
b. bully
c. cemetery
d. lobby

a. societies
d. lobby
f. tries
g. tragedy

a. valleys
b. Woodburys
tragedies
c. addresses
d. taxes
e. waltzes
f. Februarys
g. columns
h. comedies
i. ditches

es

**change the y to i
and add es—cries**

13. Write the singular forms for each word below.

a. discrepancies _____   c. cemeteries _____

b. bullies _____   d. lobbies _____

14. The endings of some words below are misspelled. By applying the rules, identify the incorrect words and spell them correctly.

a. societys _____   e. chimneys _____

b. surveys _____   f. trys _____

c. studies _____   g. tragedie _____

d. lobbie _____

REVIEW

15. Now test your skill by writing the plural noun(s) for each sentence.

a. The ranches were built only in the _____.
valley

b. The _____ have suffered many
Woodbury

_____.
tragedy

c. How many _____ does he have?
address

d. The legislature is trying to reduce _____.
tax

e. For the next orchestra concert the conductor has selected two _____.
waltz

f. Minnesota _____ are usually cold.
February

g. The auditorium has six Doric _____.
column

h. The last two Broadway hits are both _____.
comedy

i. The farmers are busy digging irrigation _____.
ditch

16. Which plural ending do you use with words ending in *s, sh, ch* (soft), *tch, s,* and *z*? _____

17. How do you form the plural of *cry*? _____

displays

18. Write the plural of *display.* _____

---

a. zoos
b. tomatoes
c. photos
d. radios
e. echoes
f. potatoes
g. Negroes
h. boos
i. vetoes
j. silos
k. heroes
l. torpedoes

19. Most nouns ending in o preceded by either a vowel or a consonant take s. Seven words, however, are exceptions: *echo, hero, Negro, potato, tomato, torpedo,* and *veto.*
Write the plurals of these "o" words.

a. zoo _____   g. Negro _____

b. tomato _____   h. boo _____

c. photo _____   i. veto _____

d. radio _____   j. silo _____

e. echo _____   k. hero _____

f. potato _____   l. torpedo _____

---

a. Negroes
b. heroes   potatoes
tomatoes
c. Echoes   vetoes
d. torpedoes

20. Perhaps an easy way to remember the exceptions is to place them in a context. Read the sentences below and supply the plural forms.

a. Some blacks prefer to be called _____.
                                                            Negro

b. The _____ like _____ and
               hero   potato

_____.
     tomato

c. _____ of the speeches condemning the gov-
     Echo
ernor's _____ rang through the corridors.
           veto

d. The twenty-year-old sailor fired the decisive _____.
                                              torpedo

---

a. silos
b. sopranos
c. potatoes
d. torpedoes
e. pianos
f. vetoes
g. bassos
h. ratios
i. Negroes
j. altos
k. rodeos
l. heroes
m. zoos
n. echoes

21. Now test your skill in writing the plurals for these words.

a. silo _____   h. ratio _____

b. soprano _____   i. Negro _____

c. potato _____   j. alto _____

d. torpedo _____   k. rodeo _____

e. piano _____   l. hero _____

f. veto _____   m. zoo _____

g. basso _____   n. echo _____

Negro
hero
potato
tomato
echo
veto
torpedo

22. Name the seven words ending in o that do not take s to form the plural.

_____   _____

_____   _____

_____   _____

a. rodeo
b. tomato
c. piano
d. veto
e. Negro
f. kangaroo
g. torpedo
h. ratio
i. hero
j. potato

23. Because it is important to spell the singular as well as the plural correctly, let us reverse the procedure and write the singular from the plural. For example, to reduce _zoos_ you simply take off the s: _zoo_. _Echoes_ has the _es_ ending, so the singular would be _echo_. Now reduce these plurals to their singular forms.

a. rodeos _____   f. kangaroos _____

b. tomatoes _____   g. torpedoes _____

c. pianos _____   h. ratios _____

d. vetoes _____   i. heroes _____

e. Negroes _____   j. potatoes _____

a. griefs
b. sheriffs
c. fifes

24. To form the plural of nouns ending in f, fe, or ff, you usually add s. For instance, the plural of _belief_ is _beliefs_, of _strife_ is _strifes_, and of _tariff_ is _tariffs_. What would be the plurals for these?

a. grief _____   c. fife _____

b. sheriff _____

a. elves
b. shelves
c. halves
d. leaves
e. thieves
f. wolves

25. Certain words ending in f or fe change their ending to ves to form the plural. Write the plurals of these words:

a. elf _____   d. leaf _____

b. shelf _____   e. thief _____

c. half _____   f. wolf _____

a. wolves
b. leaves
c. halves
d. thieves
e. elves
f. shelves

26. To remember these particular words, let us put them in a context. Read the sentence first, then supply the plural form.

a. Every night _____ roam the countryside.
                       wolf

b. In the fall trees shed their _____.
                                     leaf

c. Jack cut the apples into _____.
                                   half

d. The basement was broken into by _____.
                                         thief

e. Medieval folklore is filled with stories of _____.
   elf

f. The clerk filled the _____.
   shelf

lives
wives
knives

27. *Life*, *wife*, and *knife* are treated like the previous exceptions. How would you write the plurals of
life _____ wife _____ knife _____.

wives
lives
thieves
knives

28. Supply the plural forms.
The _____ fled for their _____ when
the _____ came after them with _____.

(under blanks: wife / life / thief / knife)

a. mischiefs
b. halves
c. wives
d. cliffs
e. leaves
f. griefs
g. lives
h. gulfs
i. strifes
j. proofs
k. sheriffs
l. thieves
m. knives
n. elves

29. Write the plurals of these words.

a. mischief _____   h. gulf _____
b. half _____   i. strife _____
c. wife _____   j. proof _____
d. cliff _____   k. sheriff _____
e. leaf _____   l. thief _____
f. grief _____   m. knife _____
g. life _____   n. elf _____

elf   elves
shelf   shelves
half   halves
leaf   leaves
thief   thieves
wolf   wolves
life   lives
wife   wives
knife   knives

30. You have studied nine words ending in *f* or *fe* that are exceptions to the general rule of adding *s* to form the plural. Write these nine words and then write their plurals. Here is *elf* as a starter.
elf _____ _____
_____ _____
_____ _____
_____ _____
_____

bacteria
media
addenda

analyses
synopses
hypotheses

31. Some nouns, Latin in origin, take the Latin plural endings. For instance, words ending in *um*, like *datum*, take *a* to form the plural: *data*. Words ending in *is*, like *crisis*, take *es* to form the plural: *crises*.
Pick out the words in this list that take the plural *a* ending and write the plurals.

bacterium _____   medium _____

analysis _____   hypothesis _____

synopsis _____   addendum _____

What are the plurals for these words:

analysis _____   synopsis _____

hypothesis _____

a. crises
b. data
hypotheses
c. analyses
d. parentheses
e. media

32. Supply the correct plural forms.

a. Almost every adult experiences several _____.
                                                          crisis

b. The educator stated that the students had not pre-sented sufficient _____ to prove their _____.
                    datum   hypothesis

c. Three scientists made separate _____
                                              analysis

of the new theory.

d. The two curved marks that indicate an inserted word in a sentence are _____.
                                        parenthesis

e. The proprietor agreed to use all the _____ of
                                                  medium

advertising.

REVIEW

s s s

33. What is the plural ending for most nouns ending in o? _____ in fe? _____ in ff? _____

a. pianos
b. beliefs
c. wives
d. potatoes
e. zoos
f. autos
g. halves
h. radios
i. Negroes
j. heroes
k. cliffs
l. griefs
m. vetoes
n. thieves
o. tariffs

34. Test your skill by writing the plurals of these nouns.

a. piano _____   i. Negro _____

b. belief _____   j. hero _____

c. wife _____   k. cliff _____

d. potato _____   l. grief _____

e. zoo _____   m. veto _____

f. auto _____   n. thief _____

g. half _____   o. tariff _____

h. radio _____

a. wish
b. potato
c. half
d. hero
e. photo
f. thief
g. kangaroo
h. life
i. Negro
j. echo

35. Write the singular form of the following plurals.

a. wishes _____   f. thieves _____

b. potatoes _____   g. kangaroos _____

c. halves _____   h. lives _____

d. heroes _____   i. Negroes _____

e. photos _____   j. echoes _____

a. hypotheses
b. bacteria
c. oases
d. media
e. bases
f. data
g. addenda
h. analyses

36. Write the plurals of these Latin words.

a. hypothesis _____   e. basis _____

b. bacterium _____   f. datum _____

c. oasis _____   g. addendum _____

d. medium _____   h. analysis _____

POSTTEST

Write the plural for these singular nouns.

1. life _____
2. switch _____
3. monarch _____
4. echo _____
5. analysis _____
6. gulch _____
7. stereo _____
8. country _____
9. shelf _____
10. addendum _____
11. photo _____
12. treaty _____
13. tomato _____
14. medium _____
15. Kennedy _____

16. company _____
17. bungalow _____
18. compress _____
19. crisis _____
20. fashion _____
21. datum _____
22. knife _____
23. deputy _____
24. family _____
25. Henry _____
26. epoch _____
27. Negro _____
28. hypothesis _____
29. lobby _____
30. wolf _____

Chapter 15

POSSESSIVES

The possessive form is an important part of spelling. And even though it has become permissible to eliminate the apostrophe or apostrophe s in some expressions, like "for consciences sake" or "at wits end," current usage still requires the use of the apostrophe in most cases of the possessive.

In working through this chapter you will recognize the singular and plural forms, apply the rules for ' or 's to a number of nouns, use the ' or 's in forming the possessives of compound nouns, distinguish between indefinite pronouns and the possessive form of the personal pronouns, and convert the possessive phrases to "of" phrases, deciding which phrases may be more euphonious. Lastly, you will become doubly aware of the possessive case and its use.

PRETEST

Write the correct form of the possessive for the nouns, compound nouns, and personal pronouns below.

1. Yesterday was the end of the _____ reign.
   king

2. Someone stole the _____ bicycles.
   boys

3. _____ catalog is not in print.
   Brannon and Butterworth
   (double ownership)

4. _____ poetry is fascinating.
   John Donne

5. The _____ reports are inaccurate.
   secretary and treasurer
   (single ownership)

6. All the _____ hats were red.
   women

7. They listened to _____ demands.
   each other

8. _____ reforms were mediocre.
   Louis the Thirteenth

9. The canary fluffed _____ feathers.
   it

10. It's strange that _____ ideas were accepted.
    nobody

11. I'm tired of listening to my _____ complaints.
    friend

12. Let me see your _____ painting.
    father-in-law

13. In the experiment a _____ delay can be crucial.
    minute

---

a. P
b. S
c. S
d. P
e. P
f. S
g. S
h. P.
....
a. 's
b. 's
c. '
d. 's
e. '
f. '
g. 's
h. 's
i. '
j. 's

1. To form the possessive we use either the apostrophe (') or the apostrophe s ('s) and the rules are simple: to nouns *not* ending in s you add 's; to plural nouns ending in s you add '. Indicate by S or P whether the following are singular or plural.

a. mice _____   e. Marys _____

b. man _____   f. boy _____

c. Harry _____   g. woman _____

d. brothers _____   h. Joneses _____

....

Indicate which form each word takes: ' or 's.

a. woman _____   f. poets _____

b. cook _____   g. women _____

c. sopranos _____   h. alto _____

d. children _____   i. queens _____

e. Baileys _____   j. Mary _____

---

a. boy's
b. tables'
c. Charles'
d. women's
e. sisters'
f. uncle's
g. friends'
h. citizen's

2. Now write the complete possessive form for these nouns.

a. boy _____   e. sisters _____

b. tables _____   f. uncle _____

c. Charles _____   g. friends _____

d. women _____   h. citizen _____

's
'

a. Harry's
b. Adams'
c. Frost's
d. students'
e. queen's
f. Joneses'
g. children's
h. church's

3. To form the possessive of nouns not ending in *s* you add _____; to plural nouns ending in *s* you add _____.

4. Read each sentence carefully, then supply the correct possessive.

a. Put _____ coat on the chair.
              Harry

b. Tom _____ name was called first.
              Adams

c. Although I like John Keats' poetry, I prefer Robert
_____.
      Frost

d. The _____ musical program was
            students
exceptional.

e. The _____ embroidered handkerchief is
          queen
missing.

f. The _____ farm is for sale.
          Joneses

g. Put the _____ names in a separate list.
          children

h. The _____ spire towered above the other
         church
buildings.

a. P
b. P
c. I
d. P
e. I
f. I P

5. Indefinite pronouns also take ' or 's for the possessive: *one's* belief, *another's* ideas, or the *others'* receipts. But the possessive forms of the personal pronoun never include the apostrophe: *his, hers, its, ours, yours, theirs*. Indicate by I or P whether the underlined are indefinite or possessive personal pronouns.

a. The bird preened <u>its</u> feathers. _____
b. I'll bring my records if you bring <u>yours</u>. _____
c. <u>Somebody's</u> hat is on the table. _____
d. I've already had my turn; now it's <u>hers</u>. _____
e. <u>Nobody's</u> suggestions were accepted. _____
f. The <u>others'</u> proposals were illogical; <u>ours</u> were not.
_____ _____

a. everybody's
b. hers
c. its

6. Now write the correct possessives for these sentences.

a. Don't believe _____ statements.
            everybody

d. others'
e. theirs
f. anybody's
g. another's

b. This is _____.
   her

c. The hawk eyed _____ prey.
   it

d. The _____ proposals are innovative.
   others

e. The property is _____.
   their

f. It's _____ guess.
   anybody

g. Many times one person's opinion is as good as _____.
   another

a. its
b. it's
c. It's
d. its

7. Remember that the contraction *it's* stands for *it is,* and that the apostrophe takes the place of the *i* in *is.* This contraction is never substituted for the possessive form of the personal pronoun. Read each sentence carefully and write the correct form: *its, it's.*

a. The dog lay on _____ back for hours.

b. I keep forgetting that _____ Monday.

c. _____ almost five o'clock.

d. Why does the tiger keep licking _____ paw?

a. law
b. secretary
   treasurer
c. lantern
d. by
e. Numeier

8. To form the possessive of a compound noun (two or more words joined together to form a single noun), you add ' or 's to the last element of the compound noun. For example, the 's would be added to *law* in *father-in-law.* In a compound expression (two or more nouns joined by a conjunction, like *Sears and Roebuck*), you add the ' or 's to the last noun to show *double* ownership (they own it together): Sears and Roebuck's catalog. For *single* ownership (each owns a share) you add ' or 's to each noun: *Mary's* and *James'* reports on ecology.
Identify the part of the underlined compound nouns or expressions that require the possessive.

a. her sister-in-law cottage _____

b. the secretary and the treasurer reports _____
   (single ownership)

c. the jack-o-lantern light _____

d. the passer-by shouts _____

e. Dunn and Numeier property _____
   (double ownership)

a. somebody else's
b. Diller and Dollar's
c. brother-in-law's
d. secretary-
   treasurer's
e. runner-up's
f. Jim's and Jean's

9. For each sentence write the complete expression in the possessive form.

a. That book is _____.
                        somebody else

b. Today I received _____
                              Diller and Dollar
                              (double ownership)

seed catalog.

c. She hung her _____
                          brother-in-law

coat on the rack.

d. We listened attentively to the _____
                                        secretary-treasurer
                                        (double ownership)

report.

e. For a while the judge could not find the _____
                                                  runner-up

medal.

f. We went to _____
                      Jim and Jean
                      (single ownership)

cafe for lunch.

a. the coat of
   Mr. Adams
b. the legs of
   the chairs
c. the dome of
   the temple
d. the coats of
   the children
e. the keys of
   the piano
f. the property
   of the Kellys
• • • • • • • • • • • • •
Your choice, but prob-
ably the legs of the
chairs, the dome of
the temple, and the
keys of the piano—
the last two particu-
larly

10. Possession can be shown by an "of" phrase as well as by the apostrophe. Although either is correct, sometimes the phrase is not only easier to use but it sounds better. For example, *the book's pages* can be expressed *the pages of the book,* and in context the second phrase may sound more euphonious than the first.

Change these possessives to phrases, watching your singular and plural forms as you do.

a. Mr. Adams' coat _____

b. the chairs' legs _____

c. the temple's dome _____

d. the children's coats _____

e. the piano's keys _____

f. the Kellys' property _____
• •
Which phrases you just wrote sound better than the possessive with the apostrophe? _____

_____

a. the semaphore's lights
b. the fans' blades
c. Tom Brown's glasses
d. the room's windows
e. the knife's edge
f. someone's proposal
• • • • • • • • • • • • •
Your choice, again. You will probably agree that at least c. and f. sound better as possessives .

11. Now convert these "of" phrases to the possessive form.

a. the lights of the semaphore _____

b. the blades of the fans _____

c. the glasses of Tom Brown _____

d. the windows of the room _____

e. the edge of the knife _____

f. the proposal of someone _____
• •
Which "of" phrase(s) do you think sound better than the possessive(s)? _____

REVIEW

a. employee's
b. Adams'
c. Secretary of Development's
d. Tim's and Tena's
e. Williams'
f. mother-in-law's
g. people's
h. its
i. mayor's and governor's
j. bosses'
k. theirs
l. Smith and Butler's

12. Now test your skill in forming possessives.

a. The supervisor criticized the _____
                              employee
work.

b. A fence separates our property from the _____.
                                        Adams

c. I doubt the veracity of the _____
                            Secretary of Development
statement.

d. _____ variety store
        Tim and Tina
     (single ownership)
closed Monday.

e. Joe _____ house is on the lakeshore.
        Williams

f. I am using my _____
                    mother-in-law
drapes.

g. He is a staunch advocate of a _____
                                  people
government.

h. The spider lured _____ prey into the web.
                      it

i. How many of the _____
                    mayor and governor
                    (single ownership)
reports do you have?

j. Both secretaries are complaining about their _____
bosses

strict rules.

k. John placed his hat on the chair; Jerry and Jim hung
_____ on the rack.
   their

l. Let's have supper at _____
Smith and Butler
(double ownership)

drugstore.

POSTTEST

Test your skill by writing the correct possessive forms.

1. Tell Mary to put _____ on the table.
   her

2. The president listened to the _____ opinions.
   others

3. From around the corner came my _____ car.
   niece

4. The council did not approve _____ suggestions.
   anyone

5. It was difficult to listen to the _____ high notes.
   sopranos

6. Let's go to _____ restaurant for dinner.
   Day and May
   (double ownership)

7. Are those your _____ overshoes?
   sisters

8. Tell them to put _____ in front.
   their

9. The bear guarded _____ cubs.
   it

10. The _____ medal was 14-carat gold.
    runner-up

11. Hanging on the wall were the _____ pictures.
    actresses

12. Gray was the color selected for the _____ hats.
    men

13. Is this _____ manuscript?
    Lucy

14. Did you ask to use your _brother-in-law's_ mower?
    brother-in-law

15. The assembly heard _Jack's_____ reports on pollution.
    Jack and Jim
    (single ownership)

Chapter 16

LY AND OUS

Do you often wonder whether to add *ly* or *ally*, and whether to change the ending of a word before adding *ous*? You need not wonder any longer, because Chapter 16 will present a few easy rules for you to follow. In this chapter you will (1) distinguish between words that take *ly* or *ally*; (2) recognize those words whose last letter must be kept, dropped, or changed before *ly* or *ous*; (3) recognize the exceptions to these rules; (4) state the reasons why pronunciation can be important in adding *ly* or *ous*; and (5) spell correctly a number of useful words in and out of context. By the end of the chapter you will be spelling such words as *publicly*, *truly*, *angrily*, *mischievous*, and *advantageous* correctly and confidently.

PRETEST

Choose the correct ending and write the complete word.

A. *ly-ally*

1. basic＿＿＿＿＿＿＿＿＿＿＿
2. moral＿＿＿＿＿＿＿＿＿＿＿
3. true＿＿＿＿＿＿＿＿＿＿＿
4. frequent＿＿＿＿＿＿＿＿＿
5. continuous＿＿＿＿＿＿＿＿
6. public＿＿＿＿＿＿＿＿＿＿
7. accidental＿＿＿＿＿＿＿＿
8. angry＿＿＿＿＿＿＿＿＿＿＿
9. chief＿＿＿＿＿＿＿＿＿＿＿
10. due＿＿＿＿＿＿＿＿＿＿＿

11. final＿＿＿＿＿＿＿＿＿＿＿
12. accurate＿＿＿＿＿＿＿＿＿
13. vague＿＿＿＿＿＿＿＿＿＿
14. whole＿＿＿＿＿＿＿＿＿＿
15. easy＿＿＿＿＿＿＿＿＿＿＿
16. coy＿＿＿＿＿＿＿＿＿＿＿
17. dry＿＿＿＿＿＿＿＿＿＿＿
18. safe＿＿＿＿＿＿＿＿＿＿＿
19. simple＿＿＿＿＿＿＿＿＿＿
20. sly＿＿＿＿＿＿＿＿＿＿＿

Add the suffix and write the complete word.

B. ous

21. vary_____   27. mountain_____

22. peril_____   28. adventure_____

23. advantage_____   29. trouble_____

24. mischief_____   30. grief_____

25. libel_____   31. victory_____

26. pity_____   32. space_____

LY-ALLY

finally

1. The general rule about forming an adverb with the suffix *ly* is to simply add *ly* after the root word. For example, *month + ly = monthly*.
Combine the root *final* and *ly*: _____.

a. frequently
b. morally
c. really
d. certainly
e. cruelly
f. accidentally
g. continuously
h. chiefly

2. Apply the rule to these roots.

a. frequent _____   e. cruel _____

b. moral _____   f. accidental _____

c. real _____   g. continuous _____

d. certain _____   h. chief _____

no—you were right
not to drop it

3. Several of the above adjectives end in the consonant *l*. Before adding *ly* did you drop the *l* at the end of the root?

_____

a. scarcely
b. duly
c. sparsely
d. truly
e. wholly
f. genuinely
g. crudely
h. simply

4. Some adjectives end in a silent e (an e that is not pronounced). Take the word *accurate* (the last sound is *t*). In adding *ly* you keep the e: *accurately*. There are four silent e words that do not keep the e: *due, true, whole,* and *simple*. Now add the suffix *ly* to the eight words below.

a. scarce _____   e. whole _____

b. due _____   f. genuine _____

c. sparse _____   g. crude _____

d. true _____   h. simple _____

whole
due
simple
true

5. From this list choose the words that drop the e before *ly*.

large	vague	simple
whole	like	true
safe	due	nice

duly
wholly
simply
truly

6. Add *ly* to the four exceptions and write the complete words.

_____   _____

_____   _____

a. b. d. f.
· · · · · · · · · · · · ·
easily
hungrily
temporarily
trickily
· · · · · · · · · · · · ·
coyly   slyly

7. Some words ending in *y* keep the *y* before *ly* and some do not. Pronounce the word *happy*. The *y* here has a long e sound (hap pee). Now pronounce the word *coy*. Here you do not have a long e sound, but a diphthong, *oy*. If a word ending in *y* has the long e sound, you drop the *y* and change it to *i* before adding *ly*: *happy* + *ly* = *happily*. If not, then you keep the *y*: *coy* + *ly* = *coyly*.
Identify which words have the long e sound of *y*:

a. easy _____   d. temporary _____

b. hungry _____   e. coy _____

c. sly _____   f. tricky _____

· ·

Write the *ly* adverbs for easy _____, hungry

_____, temporary _____,

tricky _____ .

· ·

Write the *ly* adverbs for *coy* and *sly*. _____ _____

dryly or drily
shyly or shily

8. According to the rule *dry* and *shy* do not drop the *y* (they do not have the long sound of e). Modern usage, however, permits an alternative spelling; in other words, you could change the *y* to *i* before adding *ly*.
Write the two correct spellings of both words: _____

_____   _____   _____ .

dry
shy

9. Name the two words that can be written with *y* or *i* before the *ly*: _____   _____

The *y* in each word has a long e sound.
The *y* in both words has a long *i* sound, not a long e sound.

10. The words *hungry* and *angry* change the *y* to *i* before the *ly*. Why? _____
The words *wry* and *sly* retain the *y* before the *ly*. Why?

_____

REVIEW

a. tastily
b. finally
c. extremely
d. slyly
e. wholly
f. equally

11. Test your skill in forming *ly* adverbs.

a. tasty _____   d. sly _____

b. final _____   e. whole _____

c. extreme _____   f. equal _____

g. coyly
h. duly
i. unusually
j. dryly or drily
k. truly
l. entirely
m. morally
n. gorgeously
o. simply
p. easily

g. coy	_____	l. entire	_____
h. due	_____	m. moral	_____
i. unusual	_____	n. gorgeous	_____
j. dry	_____	o. simple	_____
k. true	_____	p. easy	_____

comfortably
conceivably
profitably

12. Adjectives ending in *ble* (like *considerable*) already have the *l* in the last syllable. To form the adverb, just change the e to y. Considerable becomes considerably. What would be the adverbs for these "ble" words?

comfortable _____

conceivable _____

profitable _____

laughably
perceptibly

13. These adjectives also end in *ble*: *laughable* and *perceptible*. What are the *ly* adverbs? _____
_____

change the e to y

14. To form the *ly* adverb from an adjective ending in *ble*, what do you do? _____

ally ally
ally ly

15. To most adjectives ending in *ic* you must add *ally* instead of *ly*. To form the adverb from the adjective *basic* you add *ally*: *basically*. The one exception is the word *public*—it takes *ly*.
What is the correct suffix for each of these words (*ly, ally*)?

academic _____   genetic _____

automatic _____   public _____

a. critically
b. automatically
c. specifically
d. drastically
e. publicly

16. Now form the adverbs by adding either *ly* or *ally*.

a. He is _____ ill.
       critic

b. She moved each object _____.
       automatic

c. The proposal benefits each side _____.
       specific

d. The owner reacted _____.
       drastic

e. He announced his intentions _____.
       public

REVIEW

17. Add *ly* or *ally* as appropriate.

a. advisably
b. considerably
c. sensibly
d. basically
e. responsibly
f. publicly
g. automatically
h. reliably
i. terribly
j. apologetically
k. irritably
l. probably

a. advisable _____   g. automatic _____

b. considerable _____   h. reliable _____

c. sensible _____   i. terrible _____

d. basic _____   j. apologetic _____

e. responsible _____   k. irritable _____

f. public _____   l. probable _____

ally

18. Most words ending in *ic* add (*ly, ally*). _____

public

19. What one word ending in *ic* adds *ly*? _____

whole simple
due true

20. Most words ending in silent *e* simply add *ly* to the root. Four words are exceptions: _____ _____
_____ _____.

hungrily
y is preceded by a
consonant, so y is
changed to *i*; the y
has the long sound
of e

21. Choose the correct spelling and then state your reasons for this choice: hungryly hungrily. _____
_____

e. g.

OUS

22. Most words ending in a consonant add *ous* to form the adjective meaning full of. To the word *marvel* (which ends in the consonant *l*) you add *ous*: *marvelous*. If words end in the consonant *f*, however, you change the *f* to *v* before the *ous*. For instance, the word *grief* becomes *grievous*. Now from this list identify the words whose last consonant must be changed to *v* before adding *ous*:

a. humor _____   e. mischief _____

b. peril _____   f. hazard _____

c. danger _____   g. grief _____

d. riot _____   h. mountain _____

a. humorous
b. perilous
c. dangerous
d. riotous
e. mischievous
f. hazardous
g. grievous
h. mountainous

a. desirous
b. outrageous
c. spacious
d. adventurous
e. troublous
f. gracious

23. Add *ous* to all the words in the preceding frame.

a. _____   e. _____

b. _____   f. _____

c. _____   g. _____

d. _____   h. _____

24. Now look at and pronounce these words:

> continue   advantage   space

All end in a silent e, but the second ends in *ge* and the third in *ce*. Both the *g* and *c* have the soft sound (as in *gem* and *city*). Generally, words ending in silent e drop the e before a suffix beginning with a vowel, so before adding *ous* to a word like *continue*, you would drop the e: *continuous*. With *advantage*, you must preserve the soft sound of *g* by keeping the e: *advantageous*. Otherwise you would get the hard sound of *g* as in "advantag ous."

The soft sound of *c* presents a slightly different problem. Here you must change the e in *space*, for example, to *i*, not only to preserve the soft sound but also the pronunciation of the last syllable: "shus" in *spacious*. If you keep the e you would have to pronounce the word like this: spa   ce   ous, which, of course, is wrong.

Here are six words. Apply these guidelines and add *ous* correctly to them.

a. desire   _____   d. adventure   _____

b. outrage   _____   e. trouble   _____

c. space   _____   f. grace   _____

a. grievous
b. poisonous
c. courageous
d. libelous
e. continuous
f. spacious
g. marvelous
h. mischievous

25. Now add *ous* to this list of words.

a. grief   _____   e. continue   _____

b. poison   _____   f. space   _____

c. courage   _____   g. marvel   _____

d. libel   _____   h. mischief   _____

26. Let us look at these words:

> vary   beauty

Both end in *y*, with a consonant preceding it: an *r* in *vary* and a *t* in *beauty*. When you add a suffix beginning with a vowel, like *ous*, to words ending in *y* preceded by a consonant you usually change the *y* to *i*. *Vary* follows this rule: *various*. You cannot change the *y* in beauty to *i*, however,

a. victorious
b. plenteous
c. injurious
d. piteous

because you will change the pronunciation. The sound of the y is a long e (beautee), and to keep that sound you must change the y to e: *beauteous*. Changing the y to *i* would change the last syllable to "tious" (or "shus"), which, of course, would be wrong.
Add *ous* to these words.

a. victory _____   c. injury _____

b. plenty _____   d. pity _____

e
i

27. So as not to get the "shus" sound in pit__ous, you drop the y from *pity* and add _____. On the other hand, to keep the "shus" sound in spac__ous, you change the e to _____ and then add *ous*.

t

28. Before adding *ous* to words ending in a final y, check to see which consonant precedes the y. Change the y to e if the consonant is _____.

a. spacious
b. piteous
c. gracious

29. Add *ous* to these roots and write the complete words.

a. space _____   c. grace _____

b. pity _____

REVIEW

a. ridiculous
b. vigorous
c. gracious
d. courageous
e. mountainous
f. desirous
g. various
h. grievous
i. plenteous
j. dangerous
k. spacious
l. bounteous
m. mischievous
n. riotous
o. advantageous
p. porous

30. Now test your skill by adding *ous* to these words and writing the complete words.

a. ridicule _____   i. plenty _____

b. vigor _____   j. danger _____

c. grace _____   k. space _____

d. courage _____   l. bounty _____

e. mountain _____   m. mischief _____

f. desire _____   n. riot _____

g. vary _____   o. advantage _____

h. grief _____   p. pore _____

drop

31. In adding *ous* to *desire*, you (drop, keep) the e. _____

keep
e retains soft g.

32. In adding *ous* to *advantage*, or *courage*, you (drop, keep) the silent e. _____
State the reason why. _____

i

33. *Space* and *grace* have a soft *c*. But instead of keeping the *e*, you must change it to _____ before *ous*.

v

34. Words ending in *f* change the *f* to _____ before *ous*.

e

35. The following words end in a long *e* sound: *plenty, bounty, pity.* So that this sound is not changed before *ous*, you must drop the *y* and add _____.

POSTTEST

Add the suffix to the root word and write the complete word.

A. *ly-ally*

1. real	_____	11. academic	_____
2. angry	_____	12. entire	_____
3. true	_____	13. simple	_____
4. shy	_____	14. like	_____
5. certain	_____	15. tasty	_____
6. final	_____	16. perceptible	_____
7. public	_____	17. drastic	_____
8. hungry	_____	18. due	_____
9. apologetic	_____	19. tricky	_____
10. whole	_____	20. sly	_____

B. *ous*

21. grief	_____	27. ridicule	_____
22. desire	_____	28. bounty	_____
23. hazard	_____	29. danger	_____
24. courage	_____	30. riot	_____
25. grace	_____	31. injury	_____
26. plenty	_____	32. mischief	_____

Test
PART THREE

A. Indicate whether each sentence is true or false by writing *T* or *F* in the right-hand column.

1. The correct spelling of *study* + *ing* is *studing*. _____

2. In adding *ence* to *refer*, *prefer*, and *confer*, you double the *r* at the end of each word. _____

3. *Beginning* is spelled correctly. _____

4. In adding *able* to *pronounce*, you drop the *e*. _____

5. In each of these words—*cemetery*, *tragedy*, *inquiry*, and *county*—you change the *y* to *i* before adding *es*. _____

6. The *es* plural ending is added to *wish*, *pitch*, *tax*, and *porch*. _____

7. *Due*, *true*, *whole*, and *simple* are examples of silent *e* words that keep the *e* before *ly*. _____

8. *Panic*, *frolic*, *traffic*, and *mimic* add a *k* before *ing* and *ed*. _____

9. *Height* is not misspelled. _____

10. *Leisure*, *weird*, and *seize* are examples of the rule for the "long e" sound of the *i* and *e*. _____

11. *Echo*, *Negro*, *potato* take *s* to form the plural. _____

12. The possessive form of *women* is *womens*. _____

13. The word in italics is correctly spelled: The bird preened *its* feathers. _____

14. *Mischievious* and *grievious* are misspelled. _____

15. The possessive of *father-in-law* is *father-in-law's*. _____

16. To form the plural of *wolf*, *leaf*, and *half*, you add *s* to each word. _____

17. *Lives*, *wives*, and *knives* are correctly spelled. _____

18. The plural ending of *crisis* is *es*. _____

19. *Data* is the plural of *datum*. _____

20. The plural of *hypothesis* is *hypotheses*. _____

B. Add the specified suffix, or choose the correct suffix, and write the complete word.

21. grim   *er*   _____

22. drop   *ing*   _____

23. equip   *ed*   _____

24. begin   *ing*   _____

25. occur   *ence*   _____

26. prefer   *ence*   _____

27. lose   *ing*   _____

28. rude   *ness*   _____

29. desire   *ous*   _____

30. portray   *al*   _____

31. receive   *able*   _____

32. envoy   *s*   _____

33. discrepancy   *es*   _____

34. deny   *al*   _____

35. Kennedy   *s*   _____

36. differ   *ence*   _____

37. public   *(ally, ly)*   _____

38. critical   *(ally, ly)*   _____

39. rely   *ably*   _____

40. hungry   *ly*   _____

41. excel   *ency*   _____

42. chagrin   *ing*   _____

43. control   *ed*   _____

44. manage   *ing*   _____

45. service   *able*   _____

46. immense   *ity*   _____

47. argue   *ment*   _____

48. argue   *ing*   _____

49. society   *es*   _____

50. try   *es*   _____

51. mimic   *ry*   _____

52. equip   *age*   _____

53. gossip   *y*   _____

54. use   *age*   _____

55. frolic   *some*   _____

Final Test

A. Divide the following words into syllables.

1. incantation _____
2. commendation _____
3. auspicious _____
4. mathematical _____
5. accumulate _____

6. harassment _____
7. servitude _____
8. incalculable _____
9. biography _____
10. commemoration _____

B. Write the complete words.

11. expel *ing* _____
12. transfer *ed* _____
13. rebut *al* _____
14. benefit *ed* _____
15. grip *er* _____
16. portrait *ure* _____
17. lay *ed* _____
18. dye *ing* _____
19. copy *ing* _____
20. whole *ly* _____
21. steady *ing* _____
22. canoe *ist* _____
23. recur *ing* _____
24. nine *th* _____
25. become *ing* _____

26. argue   *ment*   _____

27. thorny   *er*   _____

28. divine   *ity*   _____

29. panic   *y*   _____

30. stingy   *ness*   _____

C. Underscore the correctly spelled word in the parentheses.

31. Zelda has a (foreign, foriegn) accent.
32. The officer chased the (theives, thieves) around the block.
33. Diana must (forfeit, forfiet) her claim.
34. The man suddenly (siezed, seized) my arm.
35. That was a (weird, wierd) story!
36. The boys held onto the (reins, riens).
37. Abbie is a (conscientious, consceintious) worker.
38. When will you (recieve, receive) the box?
39. The little child is (mischievous, mischeivous).
40. A language of historical antiquity is (Ancient, Anceint) Greek.

D. Underline the correct word in the parentheses.

41. All the students (accept, except) Joan will apply for a part-time job.
42. Nan does a (thorough, through) housecleaning.
43. What will you do (than, then)?
44. This has been (quite, quiet) a celebration.
45. The German (consul, council) matched wits with the Austrian ambassador.
46. The clerk has (access, excess) to all the storerooms.
47. Put on your gloves before you (loose, lose) them!
48. Boise is the (capitol, capital) of Idaho.
49. The (principal, principle) (affect, effect) of the demonstration was a further polarization of the factions.
50. I (past, passed) the final examination.
51. To prove your argument, there must be a (casual, causal) relationship between your points.
52. Gerald told the (personnel, personal) director that his problems had been solved.
53. Be sure to (site, cite) your sources alphabetically.
54. The mayor sought (advise, advice) from the committee.
55. To be correct in formal writing, always use (alright, all right).

E. Fill in the appropriate endings: *cede, ceed, sede.*

56. The water will soon re_____.
57. "To agree to" is the meaning of the verb ac_____.
58. Will this issue super_____ the one published last month?

59. The demand will undoubtedly ex_____ the supply.
60. She will con_____ two major points in the debate.
61. Do you think he will inter_____ for me?
62. The instructor told the group to pro_____ with the test.
63. To go before means to pre_____.
64. I don't think Pat will suc_____ Jerry as club secretary.
65. The verb that means to go before in time and space is ante_____.

F. Some italicized words are misspelled; others are not. Place a C in the right-hand column if the word is correct; if it is incorrect, write it accurately.

66. My uncle *preforms* with the opera company. _____

67. Lucy gave a vivid *discription* of her trip to Scotland. _____

68. The father's hopes turned to *despair*. _____

69. Sam *prespires* excessively. _____

70. The powder quickly *disolved* in the liquid. _____

71. I *misspelled* two words on the test. _____

72. Her screaming *unnerved* him. _____

73. It was a *mistatement* of fact. _____

74. How can I *recomend* him? _____

75. He didn't like the new *proceedure*. _____

76. There is always room for *disent*. _____

77. She *disapproved* the request. _____

78. They *destroyed* the birds' nests. _____

79. Unearned grades can be a *diservice* to the student. _____

80. Slowly they *descended* from the mountain top. _____

G. Combine the roots and suffixes and write the complete words.

81. public   *ly*   _____
82. plenty   *ous*   _____
83. true   *ly*   _____
84. pity   *ous*   _____
85. courage   *ous*   _____
86. dry   *ly*   _____
87. conceivable *ly*   _____
88. continue   *ous*   _____

89.	angry	*ly*	_____
90.	space	*ous*	_____
91.	due	*ly*	_____
92.	vary	*ous*	_____
93.	sly	*ly*	_____
94.	advantage	*ous*	_____
95.	whole	*ly*	_____

H. Underscore the correct word in the parentheses.

96. They became (heros, heroes) overnight.
97. The farmer brought us two sacks of (potatos, potatoes).
98. Quite a few (Negroes, Negros) attend our school.
99. Our neighbors have had several (tragedys, tragedies) in the past six years.
100. We received sixty (replies, replys) to the questionnaire.
101. Each group polled (it's, its', its) members.
102. There were five (bullies, bullys) in the block.
103. Some UN members specialize in (vetos, vetoes).
104. We pursued the (thiefs, thieves) for two miles.
105. It's (everybodys, everybody's) business.
106. Not all problems are (societies, society's) fault.
107. We heard (cries, crys) coming from the barn.
108. They say a cat has nine (lifes, lives).
109. Ray sat on his (mother's, mothers') hat.
110. He hasn't earned a (days, day's) pay since October.

I. Finish these definitions by completing the key words.

111. Something that hinders is a hin_____.
112. From time to time means oc_____.
113. To acknowledge or approve of is to rec_____.
114. An expert in large-scale financial affairs is called a fin_____.
115. To be similar or analogous is to be par_____.
116. Comical is a synonym for hu_____.
117. A special right or advantage is called a priv_____.
118. To be odd or strange is to be pecu_____.
119. Social and cultural conditions affecting a community are known as envi_____
_____.
120. Absurd is a synonym for r_____ulous.
121. To be acquainted with is to be fam_____ with.
122. A building to house students is known as a dor_____.
123. A natural electrical discharge in the atmosphere is called light_____.
124. A calamitous event is a tra_____.
125. Ruinous is a synonym for disas_____.

J. Choose the correct suffix and write the complete word.

126. evit   (able, ible)   _____

127. promin (ance, ence)   _____

128. surpr   (ize, ise)   _____

129. notice   (able, ible)   _____

130. digest   (able, ible)   _____

131. signific   (ant, ent)   _____

132. defend   (ant, ent)   _____

133. anal   (ize, yze)   _____

134. advert   (ize, ise)   _____

135. station   (ery, ary)   _____
     (fixed)

136. experi   (ance, ence)   _____

137. rectify   (ible, able)   _____

138. persist   (ent, ant)   _____

139. assist   (ent, ant)   _____

140. insist   (ent, ant)   _____

141. superv   (ize, ise)   _____

142. exerc   (ize, ise)   _____

143. percept   (able, ible)   _____

144. pity   (ible, able)   _____

145. abund   (ance, ence)   _____

K. Fill in the missing letters.

146. de__t

147. lon__liness

148. a__quire

149. _____claim

150. proc_____ure

151. accom_____date

152. contr__versy

153. _____gravate

154. math__matics

155. simil_____

156. ____pall
157. sent____ce
158. ben__fit
159. ____quaint
160. gover__ment
161. ath__ __ __ __
162. li__ble
163. oc____sionally
164. cat__gory
165. gram_____
166. compar__tive
167. quan____ty
168. back__round
169. ____semble
170. bull__tin

Appendixes

Appendix A

GUIDELINES FOR SYLLABICATION

To be correctly spelled, some words seem to defy rules, pronunciation or meaning guides, and about the only way to master them is to divide them into syllables. This does not mean that only these words should be syllabified; on the contrary, syllabication is a good basis for spelling many words, particularly unfamiliar ones.

Of the several methods of syllabication the one presented here is a graphic presentation, not a phonetic one. Not that sound is unimportant. Indeed it is, but to give you a phonetic system without being able to assume that you have studied linguistics would be assuming too much.

The graphic system does take pronunciation and the various characteristics of the English language into account, and because it demands some knowledge of vowel sounds, stress, and the components of words, this chapter will present the basic material as concisely as possible. You will become familiar with long and short sounds of vowels, semivowels, diphthongs, and the stress in syllables. Further, you will apply specific guidelines in the dividing of words of two or more syllables. By the end of the appendix you will confidently divide a word into its parts.

One last word: these guidelines are simply that. They are not hard and fast rules, but aids. They will, however, help you to spell correctly and to follow the syllabication in any standard dictionary. If you already know about vowels, consonants, diphthongs, stress, and the like, you can begin with frame 13. If you are unfamiliar with this material, or if you want a short refresher, start at the beginning of the Appendix.

PRETEST

Divide these words into syllables. To indicate the separation between syllables, leave a space in between: con   fer   ence.

1. necessary	_____	11. reference	_____
2. manufacture	_____	12. accumulate	_____
3. vowel	_____	13. delude	_____
4. accommodate	_____	14. pilot	_____
5. carpenter	_____	15. sophomore	_____
6. rapid	_____	16. antibody	_____
7. consideration	_____	17. consonant	_____
8. antipathy	_____	18. appearance	_____
9. geology	_____	19. tribulation	_____
10. rubble	_____	20. rivalry	_____

a. C
b. C
c. C
d. S
e. S
f. V
g. C
h. V

1. Of the twenty-six letters of the English alphabet five can be classed as vowels, three as semivowels, and the rest as consonants. The vowel sounds are represented by the letters *a, e, i, o, u*; the semivowels *w, h, y*; and the consonants by the other letters, like *b, c, d, g, s*.

Indicate by V, S, or C whether the following letters represent vowels, semivowels, or consonants.

a. s_____   c. b_____   e. h_____   g. x_____

b. p_____   d. w_____   f. e_____   h. a_____

i   o   u

2. In the preceding frame you checked *a* and *e* as vowels. You were correct. Name the other three: _____

y

3. You checked *w* and *h* as semivowels, and again you were correct. What is the third semivowel? _____

a   e   i   o   u
w   h   y

4. List all the vowels and semivowels: _____
_____.

b.   d.   e.   g.   h.

5. Identify the consonants.

a. a_____   c. u_____   e. b_____   g. f_____

b. g_____   d. s_____   f. h_____   h. k_____

6. For the vowels there are long and short sounds and diphthongs. The long sounds are usually higher, longer, and tenser than the short sounds. Pronounce these words: *bite* and *bit*. Yes, the *i* in *bite* is higher, longer, and tenser than the *i* in *bit*, so it is the long sound. Since the *i* in *bit* is not nearly as long, high, or tense, it is the short sound. Diphthongs are speech sounds moving from one vowel to another vowel or to a semivowel within the same syllable. Take the words *boil* and *toy*. Pronounce them slowly—the vowels *oi* and the vowel *o* and semivowel *y* blend together. Pronounce these two groups of words, then answer this question: Which group has the long sound of the vowels?

_____

A.	B.
Pete	bit
rate	top
beet	met
proof	hat
stone	but
night	knit
rude	rut

• •

Do the underlined portions in these words qualify as diphthongs? _____

spout   plow

7. Now identify whether the underlined portions are long or short vowels, or diphthongs. Use L, S, or D as indicators.

a. bitter _____   d. frame _____

b. key _____   e. pout _____

c. boil _____   f. butter _____

8. Sometimes two vowel letters result in a long vowel sound. To distinguish between the long vowel and the diphthong remember that a long sound is *one* sound, whereas a diphthong is a *movement* from one vowel sound to another or to a semivowel. Here are two words: *freight* and *mate*. Both have the long *a* sound. In the first, two vowels (ei) constitute the single sound; in the second, the single vowel *a*. In the words *toil* (two vowels) or *boy* (vowel and semivowel) you have diphthongs as there is a movement from *o* to *i* and from *o* to *y*.

a. L
b. D
c. L
d. L
e. L
f. D
g. L
h. D

Pronounce each word below, then identify whether the underlined portion is a long sound (L) or a diphthong (D).

a. believe _____ e. meat _____

b. boisterous _____ f. poise _____

c. boat _____ g. main _____

d. reindeer _____ h. plow _____

a. C
b. V
c. C
d. V
e. D
f. V
g. C
h. D

9. The *semi* in semivowel suggests that they are and they are not vowels. This is correct because in most systems of classification *w*, *h*, and *y* are included with the consonants but are acknowledged as being capable of producing vowel sounds. As consonants they precede vowels, as in *way*, *you*, and *he*; as vowels they usually follow a simple vowel to help make a long vowel sound: *tow* or a diphthong: *ploy*. The *y* can also be a full vowel with the long sound of *e*. If you pronounce *skinny* or *clammy*, you will hear the long e sound of *y*; its function, of course, is to serve as a suffix (or ending).

Now check which sound the underlined portions produce: C (consonant), V (vowel), and D (diphthong).

a. hoe _____ e. boy _____

b. lawyer _____ f. they _____

c. wide _____ g. yea _____

d. low _____ h. cow _____

long e
suffix (or ending)

10. Now pronounce these words:

gossipy   chunky   happy

What sound does the *y* have? _____

What is the function of the *y*? _____

11. There are several technical ways to define a syllable and its components, but suffice it to say that a syllable is the smallest phonological construction and usually consists of a pronounced vowel or diphthong or either one or more vowels with one or more consonants. Let us also say that a syllable can form a complete word or is part of a larger word. For instance, the word *bat* has one pronounced vowel (*a*) which is preceded by and followed by one consonant (*b* and *t*). The sounds produce just one syllable, in this case a complete word. Often such a word is called a one-syllable word. Now take the word *plow*— it has a diphthong instead of a single vowel—but together with the consonants *pl* it forms one syllable, and again a complete word.

a. 2
b. 3
c. 1
d. 2
e. 2
f. 5
g. 1
h. 3
i. 2

If you add a suffix to a word, like *er* to *bat,* you get *batter.* Here you have two pronounced vowels (*a* and *e*) forming two syllables: bat ter. Root words, those words without any additions (prefixes or suffixes), can have more than one syllable, for example: *garden, loiter, establish.* In each word you have several pronounced vowels or diphthongs: *gar* den *loi* ter *es* tab *lish.* Sometimes a consonant can form a syllable without a vowel (called a syllabic consonant). Pronounce these words: *riddle, bottle.* Each has two syllables *rid dle bot tle,* with the second syllable having just an "l" sound.

In summing up, we can say that a syllable consists of either a vowel or a diphthong alone, a syllabic consonant, or either one or the other with one or more consonants. Now say the following words carefully, looking at and hearing the vowels. Then indicate the number of syllables in each.

a. summer _____   f. considerable _____

b. consonant _____   g. coat _____

c. hoe _____   h. disapprove _____

d. vowel _____   i. battle _____

e. shepherd _____

a. clámmy
b. repeĺ
c. none
d. accómmodate
e. páddle
f. cońsonant
g. preseŕve
h. none

12. One last point to consider before studying the guidelines is the stress. Stress (or accent) is the prominence which develops from pronouncing one or more syllables more strongly than the other(s). One-syllable words have no stress, so let us turn to multisyllabic words. *Garden,* for instance, has two syllables and in pronouncing it you stress the first syllable: gaŕ den. In *establish* you stress the second: es tab́ lish. In the word *consideration,* however, you have more than one stress resulting in what we call "major" (´) and "minor" (´) stress: con sid er á tion. But remember, there is never more than one major stress in a word.

Now indicate the stress or stresses in these words. Use the same marks shown above: the bold mark for major, a similar but lighter mark for minor. If the word has no accent indicate "none."

a. clammy _____   e. paddle _____

b. repel _____   f. consonant _____

c. course _____   g. preserve _____

d. accommodate _____   h. club _____

a. vowels
b. long
c. is

13. Now we are ready for the guidelines. If a single con-sonant comes between two vowels, the first of which has a *long* sound and is *accented*, the consonant will usually go with the *second* vowel. Look at and pronounce *pilot*. The single consonant *l* comes between two vowels *i* and *o*. The first vowel has the long sound of *i* and carries the stress (pí lot). The consonant *l* will therefore go with the second vowel: pi lot.

Now pronounce the word *garden*. It has the stress on the first vowel, but between the two vowels (*a* and *e*) come two consonants (*r* and *d*). We cannot apply this guideline to this word. How about *money?* Again we have two vowels (*o* and *e*) and a single consonant (*n*) between the two vowels, but the first vowel (*o*) does not have the long sound. So this word cannot be divided like pilot. To divide words like pilot we must look for these requirements:

a. it must have a single consonant between two _____.

b. the first vowel must have a (long, short) sound. _____

c. the first vowel (is, is not) stressed. _____

a. no
b. yes
c. no
d. yes
e. no
f. no

14. For each two-syllable word below, write yes or no to indicate whether it would be divided like pilot.

a. compel _____   d. local _____

b. native _____   e. rusty _____

c. dollar _____   f. palace _____

a. 1 and 2
b. 1 and 3
c. 1 and 3
d. 3

15. *Native* and *local* are syllabified like pilot as they meet all the requirements. For the rest of the words in the above list, write the number of the reason(s) for their not meet-ing the requirements.
1. two consonants between two vowels
2. stress on second syllable
3. short sound of first vowel
4. a vowel between two consonants

a. compel _____   c. rusty _____

b. dollar _____   d. palace _____

a. fi   nal
b. na   tive
c. lo   cal
d. ri   val
e. fa   vor

16. Now divide these words into syllables, leaving a space to indicate the separation: pi lot.

a. final _____   d. rival _____

b. native _____   e. favor _____

c. local _____

do

17. We are ready for the second guideline: when a consonant comes between vowels, the first of which is *short* and *accented*, the consonant will usually go with the *first* vowel. *Modest* is a good example. The *d* comes between the *o* and *e*, the first vowel has a short sound of *o* and is accented, so the *d* goes with the first vowel (*o*) to form the first syllable: mod est. Pronounce these words:

palace   solid   ravel   tepid

They (do, do not) meet this guideline. _____

a. pal	ace
b. sol	id
c. rav	el
d. tep	id

18. Now divide the following into syllables.

a. palace _____   c. ravel _____

b. solid _____   d. tepid _____

a. ro	bust
b. rap	id
c. ten	or
d. me	ter
e. mon	ey
f. pu	pil
g. bo	nus
h. del	uge

19. Test your skill by applying the guidelines presented thus far to these words.

a. robust _____   e. money _____

b. rapid _____   f. pupil _____

c. tenor _____   g. bonus _____

d. meter _____   h. deluge _____

a. pot	ter
b. jag	ged
c. pon	der
d. gos	sip
e. med	dle
f. hur	tle
g. car	pet
h. gin	ger

20. Here is the third guideline: if a word has two consonants between two vowels, you usually divide between the consonants. For instance, in *garden* the *rd* comes between *a* and *e*. To divide you would separate the *r* and *d*: gar den. If a word ends in *le* the consonant preceding the *le* usually combines with the *le* to form a syllable. Take the word *turtle*. It ends in *le*, so the consonant immediately preceding it (*t*) goes with the *le* to form the second syllable: tur tle.
Keeping these guidelines in mind, divide the following:

a. potter _____   e meddle _____

b. jagged _____   f. hurtle _____

c. ponder _____   g. carpet _____

d. gossip _____   h. ginger _____

21. As far as possible try to syllabify a word according to its structure, but always keep the pronunciation in mind. If the word contains a prefix (an element added to the beginning of a word), and this prefix sounds out a syllable, separate it from the root word: *dis* approve, *re* fer. Let us look at these words: *misspell, disappoint, antibody*. Each has a prefix (*mis, dis, anti*), so it can be separated from

a. pre   fer
b. dis   miss
c. pro   ceed
d. dis   ap   pear
e. per   form
f. an   tith   e   sis

the root. But there is a difference: *mis* and *dis* have one syllable and *anti* has two. The proper syllabication then would be *mis* spell, *dis* ap point, *an ti* bod y. Here is another *anti*: *antipathy*. The prefix in this word is not pronounced the same as in *antibody*, so in *antipathy* the pronunciation must be followed for syllabication:

an   ti   bod y   but   an   tip   a   thy

Say the following words aloud, then syllabify them.

a. prefer _____   d. disappear _____

b. dismiss _____   e. perform _____

c. proceed _____   f. antithesis _____

a. *ly*
b. *ness*
c. *ful*   *ness*
d. *y*
e. *ence*

22. You should also be able to distinguish suffixes (elements at the end of words) from the roots. For instance, *helpful*, *entirely*, and *consolable* each have a suffix: *ful*, *ly*, and *able*. Again we have two (*ful* and *ly*) that have one syllable each, and *able* that has two.
For the following words identify the suffix in each word. Remember that words can have more than one suffix.

a. happily _____   d. grumpy _____

b. trueness _____   e. existence _____

c. helpfulness _____

a. hap   pi   ly
b. true   ness
c. help   ful   ness
d. grum   py
e. ex   is   tence

23. Let us take the same words in frame 22 to syllabify. You have identified the suffixes, so now, remembering your guidelines, pronounce the words carefully and write the syllables.

a. happily _____   d. grumpy _____

b. trueness _____   e. existence _____

c. helpfulness _____

2 consonants (st)
between 2 vowels
(*i*   e)

24. Even though *existence* has a suffix (*ence*) why do you divide between the *st* for the second and third syllables:

_____

REVIEW

a. del uge
b. stu pid
c. por tal
d. dou ble
e. de lude
f. pos ture
g. re vise
h. doubt ful
i. stum ble
j. hub bub
k. jum bo

25. Test your skill by dividing these words into syllables. Remember that pronunciation and stress are important.

a. deluge _____   g. revise _____

b. stupid _____   h. doubtful _____

c. portal _____   i. stumble _____

d. double _____   j. hubbub _____

e. delude _____   k. jumbo _____

f. posture _____

second

26. When a single consonant comes between two vowels, the first of which is long and accented (*local*) the consonant usually goes with the (first, second) vowel. _____

first

27. When a single consonant comes between two vowels, the first of which is short and accented (*palace*), the consonant usually goes with the (first, second) vowel. _____

le

28. If a word ends in *le*, the consonant preceding it goes with the _____ to form a syllable.

between

29. If two consonants come between two vowels, you usually divide _____ the consonants.

3
first
soph o more

30. Now that you have these guidelines firmly in mind, let us take longer words. How about *accommodate*. Because there are four pronounced vowels you can assume that there are four syllables. If you look closely at the word you will see two double consonants: *cc* and *mm*, both between vowels. You can divide between these double consonants: ac com modate. The last part can be divided after the long sound of *o* (in modate) and thus you have the four syllables: ac com mo date.

The word *sophomore* is also a good word to syllabify. How many pronounced vowels does it have? _____ Coming as it does from the Greek, it has the *ph* sounding like the single consonant *f*. Does the *ph* go with the first or second vowel? _____ Now divide it into syllables.

a. per fec tion
b. com mit tee
c. prep a ra tion
d. ar gu ment
e. suc ces sion
f. spec i men

31. Here are some multisyllabic words to divide. Pronounce them carefully and then apply the guidelines.

a. perfection _____   d. argument _____

b. committee _____   e. succession _____

c. preparation _____   f. specimen _____

a. car pen ter
b. es tab lish
   ment
c. dis crim i
   nate
d. lib er al
e. ac cu mu
   late
f. du pli cate
g. nec es sar y
h. in ef fec tive

32. Below is a list of questions to remind you of the guidelines for syllabication.
Is there a vowel between two consonants?
Is the first vowel long or short?
Are there two consonants between two vowels?
Is there a prefix or suffix in the word?
Does the word end in *le*?
Using these questions as reminders, divide the following words. Don't forget to pronounce them.

a. carpenter _____ e. accumulate _____

b. establishment _____ f. duplicate _____

c. discriminate _____ g. necessary _____

d. liberal _____ h. ineffective _____

POSTTEST

Divide these words into syllables. To indicate the separation, leave a space in between: gar den er.

1. controversy _____
2. restaurant _____
3. recurrence _____
4. precede _____
5. disappointment _____
6. tremendous _____
7. unnecessary _____
8. description _____
9. opportunity _____
10. advantageous _____
11. incidental _____
12. documentary _____
13. knowledge _____
14. Wednesday _____
15. psychology _____
16. ridiculous _____
17. achievement _____
18. forgotten _____
19. government _____
20. procedure _____

Appendix B

TEST ANSWERS

DIAGNOSTIC TEST

SECTION A

1. mischievous
2. descriptive
3. C
4. C
5. category
6. surprise
7. C
8. precede
9. principle
10. lose
11. C
12. C
13. interest
14. rhythm
15. dormitory
16. C
17. expressible
18. C
19. C
20. C
21. athletics
22. unnecessary
23. C
24. guardian
25. definite
26. C
27. C
28. proceed
29. its
30. C
31. wondrous
32. misstated
33. possession
34. C
35. similar
36. noticeable
37. cemetery
38. C
39. passed
40. quiet
41. remembrance
42. recommend
43. explanation
44. C
45. separation
46. C
47. C
48. C
49. it's
50. C
51. temperament
52. performed
53. acquire
54. C
55. C
56. defendant
57. analyze
58. C
59. too
60. casual

SECTION B

1. equipped
2. benefiting
3. ninth
4. desirous
5. C
6. C
7. vetoes
8. C
9. wholly
10. adventurous
11. beginning
12. C
13. becoming
14. writing
15. C
16. seize
17. copies
18. ours
19. drastically
20. advantageous
21. C
22. tonnage
23. C
24. C
25. studying
26. friendship
27. calves
28. C
29. C
30. C
31. omitted
32. occurrence
33. ninety
34. C
35. C
36. C
37. thieves
38. C
39. practically
40. C
41. C
42. conferring
43. density
44. C
45. tries
46. C
47. echoes
48. women's
49. lonely
50. C
51. C
52. equipage
53. owing
54. C
55. pitiful
56. ancient
57. potato
58. hers
59. C
60. spacious

CHAPTER 1 PRONUNCIATION AND ENUNCIATION

PRETEST
1. hindrance
2. recognize
3. athlete
4. mischievous
5. lightening
6. tragedy
7. chimney
8. temperature
9. athletics
10. liable
11. finally
12. disastrous
13. vegetable
14. lightning
15. prejudice
16. federal
17. remembrance
18. grievous
19. temperament
20. quantity
21. government
22. environment
23. background
24. gratitude
25. hundred
26. aggravate

If you had 23 of 26 correct, you may bypass this chapter. But before you do, find your wrong answer numbers (if any) below, and read the corresponding frames in the chapter so that you will not misspell any words in this test.

Answer numbers	Frames	Answer numbers	Frames
1, 3, 4, 5, 7, 9, 12, 14, 17, 18	1–25	11, 20, 21, 22, 23	38–55
10, 16	27–34	2, 6, 15, 24, 25, 26	58–78
8, 13, 19	35–37		

POSTTEST
1. temperature
2. athlete
3. grievous
4. federal
5. remembrance
6. vegetable
7. environment
8. chimney
9. quantity
10. liable
11. temperament
12. hundred
13. aggravate
14. prejudice
15. recognize
16. lightning
17. disastrous
18. mischievous
19. athletics
20. lightening
21. hindrance
22. background
23. tragedy
24. finally
25. government
26. gratitude

For any wrong answers check the frames below and reread that part of the program. You do not want to leave this chapter without spelling every word correctly.

Answer numbers	Frames	Answer numbers	Frames
2. 3, 18, 19	1–7	9, 24	38–44
5, 17, 21	8–18	7, 22, 25	45–55
8, 16, 20	19–25	12, 13, 15, 26	58–73
4, 10	27–34	14, 23	74–78
1, 6, 11	35–37		

CHAPTER 2 PREFIXES

PRETEST
A.
1. disseminate
2. misspell
3. unnecessary
4. affirm
5. recollect
6. aggression
7. dissent
8. acquaint
9. mistake
10. dissect
11. unnatural
12. recommend
13. acquire

B.
14. perform
15. prepare
16. disservice
17. proceed
18. precede
19. decide
20. proscribe
21. describe
22. prescribe

If you spelled 20 of 22 correctly, you may bypass this chapter. But before you do, find your wrong answer numbers (if any) below and read the corresponding frames in the chapter so that you will not misspell any words in this test.

Answer numbers	Frames	Answer numbers	Frames
7, 10, 19, 21	1–4	1, 2, 3, 9, 11, 16	16
14, 15, 17, 18, 20, 22	5–8	4, 6	17–25
5, 12	11–15	8, 13	26–28

POSTTEST

1. perspire
2. prescription
3. persuaded
4. despair
5. prefer
6. permeated
7. describe
8. proceed
9. dissect
10. permission
11. down
12. through
13. apart
14. back
15. through
16. not
17. off (or away)
18. before
19. away (or off)
20. not
21. ad
22. appoint
23. acquaintance
24. attract
25. acquit
26. administered
   assembly

For any wrong answers check the frame references below and reread that part of the program. You do not want to leave this chapter without spelling every word in the test correctly.

Answer numbers	Frames	Answer numbers	Frames
4, 7, 11, 13, 16, 17, 19, 20	1–4	21, 22, 24, 26	17–25
1, 2, 3, 5, 6, 8, 10, 12, 15, 18	5–8	23, 25	26–28
14	11–15		
9	16		

CHAPTER 3   SYLLABICATION

PRETEST

1. interest
2. embarrass
3. irrelevant
4. sergeant
5. villain
6. experience
7. acquire
8. immediately
9. dissatisfaction
10. vacuum
11. apparent
12. convenience
13. procedure
14. occasionally
15. disappoint
16. loneliness
17. opportunity
18. financier
19. discrimination
20. parallel
21. accumulate
22. disappear
23. interrupt
24. restaurant
25. appreciate
26. acquaintance
27. explanation
28. accomplishment
29. possession

If you had 26 of 29 correct, you may bypass this chapter. But before you do, find your wrong answer numbers, if any, below and read the corresponding frames in the chapter so that you will not misspell any words in this test.

Answer numbers	Frames	Answer numbers	Frames
11, 14, 17, 21, 25, 28	1–15	13, 27	57–61
9, 15, 19, 22	17–25	6, 12	63–71
2, 8, 20, 29	26–39	5	72–74
7, 26	41–44	1, 10	75–80
3, 16, 23	45–56	4, 18, 24	81–88

POSTTEST

1. vacuum	9. immediately	17. opportunity	25. explanation
2. villain	10. procedure	18. convenience	26. accomplishment
3. interest	11. occasionally	19. interrupt	27. parallel
4. sergeant	12. loneliness	20. acquaintance	28. possession
5. embarrass	13. financier	21. dissatisfaction	29. irrelevant
6. acquire	14. apparent	22. restaurant	
7. disappear	15. discrimination	23. appreciate	
8. experience	16. accumulate	24. disappoint	

For any wrong answer(s) check the frame references below and reread that part of the program. You do not want to leave this chapter without spelling every word in the test correctly.

Answer numbers	Frames	Answer numbers	Frames
11, 14, 16, 17, 23, 26	1–15	10, 25	57–61
7, 15, 21, 24	17–25	8, 18	63–71
5, 9, 27, 28	26–39	2	72–74
6, 20	41–44	1, 3	75–80
12, 19, 29	45–56	4, 13, 22	81–88

CHAPTER 4 SILENT LETTERS

PRETEST

1. Wednesday	5. psychology	9. exhaust	13. psychiatry
2. debt	6. rhythm	10. guard	14. doubt
3. condemn	7. knowledge	11. subtle	
4. guardian	8. undoubtedly	12. writer	

If you had 12 of 14 correct, you may bypass this chapter. But before you do, find any wrong answers (if any) below, and read the corresponding frames in the chapter so that you will not misspell any word in this test.

Answer numbers	Frames	Answer numbers	Frames
2, 8, 11, 14	1–3	3	22–27
1	4–7	5, 13	28–32
6, 9	8–16	4, 10	33–36
7	17–20	12	37–41

POSTTEST

1. guard	5. Wednesday	9. condemn	13. exhaust
2. writing	6. rhythm	10. guardian	14. writer
3. psychology	7. knowledge	11. subtle	15. psychiatry
4. doubt	8. debt	12. undoubtedly	

For any wrong answer(s) check the frame references below and reread that part of the program. You do not want to leave this chapter without spelling every word in the test correctly.

Answer numbers	Frames	Answer numbers	Frames
4, 8, 11, 12	1–3	9	22–27
5	4–7	3, 15	28–32
6, 13	8–16	1, 10	33–36
7	17–20	2, 14	37–41

CHAPTER 5   VOWEL STRESS

PRETEST
1. benefit
2. grammar
3. optimism
4. familiar
5. humorous
6. comparative
7. ridiculous
8. eliminate
9. similar

10. dominant
11. warrant
12. candidate
13. sentence
14. mandatory
15. dormitory
16. mathematics
17. sacrifice
18. controversy

19. opinion
20. criticism
21. separate
22. definite
23. calendar
24. legitimate
25. category
26. divide
27. probably

28. fascinate
29. particular
30. privilege
31. laboratory
32. peculiar
33. bulletin
34. intelligence

If you had 30 of 34 correct, you may bypass this chapter. But before you do, find your wrong answers (if any) below, and read the corresponding frames in the chapter so that you will not misspell any words in this test.

Answer numbers	Frames	Answer numbers	Frames
7, 26	1–7	6, 14, 21, 27	31–41
11, 19, 29	8–17	1, 16, 25, 33	42–44
2, 9, 23	18–22	5, 18, 31	45–48
4, 32	23–26	3, 8, 10, 12, 15,	50–76
13	27–28	17, 20, 22, 24, 28,	
		30, 34	

POSTTEST
1. benefit
2. dormitory
3. opinion
4. sacrifice
5. peculiar
6. sentence
7. humorous
8. definite
9. criticism

10. warrant
11. laboratory
12. candidate
13. ridiculous
14. calendar
15. probably
16. bulletin
17. legitimate
18. mandatory

19. familiar
20. comparative
21. category
22. dominant
23. divide
24. grammar
25. mathematics
26. controversy
27. fascinate

28. optimism
29. separate
30. privilege
31. similar
32. particular
33. eliminate
34. intelligence

For any wrong answer(s) check the frame references below and reread that part of the program. You do not want to leave this chapter without spelling every word in the test correctly.

Answer numbers	Frames	Answer numbers	Frames
13, 23	1–7	7, 11, 26	45–48
3, 10, 32	8–17	8, 22	50–54
14, 24, 31	18–22	12, 17, 27, 33	55–62
5, 19	23–26	9, 28	63–67
6	27–28	2	68–70
15, 18, 20, 29	31–41	34	71–73
1, 16, 21, 25	42–44	4, 30	74–76

CHAPTER 6   SOUND-ALIKE SUFFIXES

PRETEST
A. *able-ible*
1. permissible
2. acceptable
3. estimable
4. changeable

5. admirable
6. marketable
7. inevitable
8. eligible

9. considerable
10. passable
11. possible
12. perishable

13. defensible
14. repressible
15. reducible
16. educable

B. *ary-ery*
1. boundary
2. stationery
3. secretary
4. library
5. cemetery
6. February
7. contemporary
8. stationary

C. *ise-ize-yze*
1. advise
2. analyze
3. criticize
4. summarize
5. surprise
6. emphasize
7. paralyze
8. exercise
9. advertise
10. realize

D. *ance-ence* (ant-ent)
1. intelligent
2. resistance
3. equivalent
4. accident
5. defendant
6. prominence
7. existent
8. confidence
9. science
10. consequent
11. experience
12. magnificence
13. maintenance
14. excellent
15. guidance
16. influence
17. extravagance
18. insistent
19. attendance
20. dominant
21. prevalence
22. **delinquent**
23. brilliance
24. significant

If you had 14 of 16 in A, 7 of 8 in B, 9 of 10 in C, and 21 of 24 in D correct, you may bypass this chapter. But before you do, find your wrong answer numbers (if any) below, and read the corresponding frames in the chapter so that you will not misspell any words in this test.

Answer numbers	Frames	Answer numbers	Frames
A.		C.	
2, 6, 9, 12	1	1, 5, 8, 9	43–51
3, 5	4–6	2, 7	52–56
7	7–8	3, 4, 6, 10	57–68
1, 10, 11, 14	9–10		
13	12–14	D.	
4, 8, 15, 16	16–19	2, 7, 18	70–73
		1, 12, 17, 24	74–76
B.		3, 6, 13, 14, 20, 21	78–80
2, 5	32–34	4, 5, 8, 15, 19, 22	82–84
8	35–36	9, 10, 11, 16, 23	85–88
1, 3, 4, 6, 7	36–37		

POSTTEST

A. *ary-ery*
1. contemporary
2. stationary
3. boundary
4. cemetery
5. February
6. secretary
7. library
8. stationery

B. *ise-ize-yze*
1. arise
2. supervise
3. characterize
4. analyze
5. surprise
6. recognize
7. advise
8. exercise
9. criticize
10. paralyze
11. realize
12. summarize

C. *able-ible*
1. multipliable
2. enforceable
3. perfectible
4. enjoyable
5. admissible
6. responsible
7. commendable
8. legible
9. corruptible
10. revocable
11. kissable
12. horrible
13. consolable
14. irritable
15. intelligible
16. dispensable

D. *ance-ence* (ant-ent)
1. science
2. convenience
3. dependent
4. importance
5. dominance
6. extravagant
7. abundance
8. resistance
9. persistence
10. attendance
11. balance
12. adolescent

13. significance	16. defendant	19. excellence	22. guidance
14. delinquent	17. maintenance	20. brilliant	23. affluent
15. competent	18. relevant	21. permanent	24. emergence

For any wrong answer(s) check the frame references below and reread that part of the program. You do not want to leave this chapter without spelling every word in the test correctly.

Answer numbers	Frames	Answer numbers	Frames
A.		**C.**	
4, 8	32–34	7, 12	1
1, 3, 5, 6, 7	35–36	1, 4	2–3
2	36–37	3, 5, 9, 13, 14	4–6
		5, 11	9–11
B.		6, 16	12–14
1, 5, 8	43–48	2, 8, 10, 15	16–19
2, 7	49–51		
4, 10	52–56	**D.**	
11	57–60	4, 8, 9, 15, 18	70–73
6, 9	61–65	6, 12, 13, 24	74–76
3, 12	66–68	5, 11, 17, 19, 21	78–80
		3, 7, 10, 16, 22	82–84
		1, 2, 14, 23	85–86
		20	87–88

TEST   PART ONE

A.

1. existence	14. dominance	27. commendable	40. library
2. relevance	15. confidence	28. educable	41. recognize
3. dependence	16. destructible	29. irritable	42. arise
4. adolescence	17. changeable	30. imaginable	43. realize
5. experience	18. admissible	31. creamery	44. paralyze
6. maintenance	19. employable	32. dictionary	45. advise
7. persistence	20. reliable	33. cemetery	46. emphasize
8. insistence	21. noticeable	34. stationery	47. criticize
9. intelligence	22. eligible	35. contemporary	48. advertise
10. magnificence	23. corruptible	36. boundary	49. surprise
11. consequence	24. dispensable	37. secretary	50. analyze
12. convenience	25. responsible	38. customary	
13. competence	26. possible	39. stationary	

B.

51. promotion	56. destroyed	61. projects	66. preface
52. despair	57. performance	62. distract	67. propensity
53. permission	58. decided	63. perspires	68. declassified
54. disease	59. prescribe	64. discredit	69. disarm
55. pertain	60. progress	65. predictions	70. presentiments

C.

71. definite	75. accommodate	79. vacuum	83. accumulated
72. C	76. aggressive	80. C	84. recommend
73. grammar	77. C	81. temperature	85. loneliness
74. C	78. C	82. C	86. lightning

87. C	91. C	95. C	99. privilege
88. C	92. mischievous	96. prejudice	100. C.
89. warrant	93. acquire	97. embarrass	
90. C	94. rhythm	98. C	

CHAPTER 7   THE "SEED" ROOTS

PRETEST
A.

1. accede	4. secede	7. antecede	10. intercede
2. proceed	5. exceed	8. recede	
3. concede	6. succeed	9. supersede	

B.

11. supersede	14. precede	17. exceed	20. recede
12. accede	15. succeed	18. secede	
13. proceed	16. intercede	19. concede	

If you had 18 of 20 correct, you may bypass this chapter. But before you do, find your wrong answers (if any) below, and read the corresponding frames in the chapter so that you will not misspell any words in this test.

Answer numbers	Frames	Answer numbers	Frames
9, 11	2–4	1, 3, 4, 7, 8, 10, 12,	10–33
2, 5, 6, 13, 15, 17	5–7	14, 16, 18, 19, 20	

POSTTEST
A.

1. recede	4. concede	7. supersede	10. antecede
2. exceed	5. accede	8. secede	
3. precede	6. proceed	9. succeed	

B.

11. succeed	14. accede	17. exceed	20. succeed
12. proceed	15. precede	18. intercede	
13. recede	16. supersede	19. concede	

For any wrong answer(s) check the frame references below and reread that part of the program. You do not want to leave this chapter without spelling every word in the test correctly.

Answer numbers	Frames	Answer numbers	Frames
7, 15	2–4	4, 5, 13, 18	18–20
2, 6, 9, 11, 16	5–7	17	23–28
3, 14	12–14	10	29
1, 12	15–17	8	33

CHAPTER 8   HOMONYMS

PRETEST

1. compliment	5. coarse	9. stationery	13. too
2. there	6. principal	10. capitol	14. their
3. already	7. council	11. cite	15. site
4. its	8. altogether	12. passed	16. capital

If you had 14 of 16 correct, you may bypass this chapter. But before you do, find your wrong answers (if any) below, and read the corresponding frames in the chapter so that you will not misspell any words in this test.

Answer numbers	Frames	Answer numbers	Frames
3	1–5	11, 15	34–36
8	6–8	2, 4, 14	38–41
10, 16	13–19	13	42–44
6	20–23	12	48–50
9	24–29	1	51–52
5	30–33	7	53–55

POSTTEST

1. complement	5. all together	9. Capitol	13. consul
2. its	6. counsel	10. to	14. They're
3. past	7. sight	11. already	15. Whose
4. course	8. stationary	12. its	16. principle

For any wrong answer(s) check the frame references below and reread that part of the program. You do not want to leave this chapter without spelling every word in the test correctly.

Answer numbers	Frames	Answer numbers	Frames
11	1–5	7	34–36
5	6–8	2, 12, 14, 15	38–41
9	13–19	10	42–44
16	20–23	3	48–50
8	24–29	1	51–52
4	30–33	6, 13	53–55

CHAPTER 9   SIMILAR WORDS

PRETEST

1. quite	5. prophesy	9. thorough	13. loose
2. access	6. accept	10. weather	
3. lose	7. than	11. personnel	
4. casual	8. effects	12. advise	

If you had 11 of 13 correct, you may bypass this chapter. But before you do, find your wrong answers (if any) below, and read the corresponding frames in the chapter so that you will not misspell any words in this test.

Answer numbers	Frames	Answer numbers	Frames
2	1–4	3, 13	25–27
4	5–8	1	28–32
8	9–12	7	34–37
5	13–17	9	38–41
6	18–19	11	42–45
12	21–24	10	46–49

POSTTEST

1. quiet	5. excess	9. prophecy	13. advice
2. whether	6. causal	10. effect	
3. personal	7. accepts	11. then	
4. loose	8. effects	12. whether	

For any wrong answer(s) check the frame references below and reread that part of the program. You do not want to leave this chapter without spelling every word in the test correctly.

Answer numbers	Frames	Answer numbers	Frames
5	1–4	4	25–27
6	5–8	1	28–32
8, 10	9–12	11	34–37
9	13–17	3	42–45
7	18–19	2, 12	46–49
13	21–24		

TEST   PART TWO

A.

1. recede
2. intercede
3. secede
4. proceed
5. concede
6. precede
7. supersede
8. succeed
9. accede
10. exceed

B.

11. effect
12. whether
13. capital
14. than
15. council
16. advise
17. lose
18. principal
19. passed
20. too
21. its
22. course
23. know
24. consul
25. Who's
26. already
27. personnel
28. accept
29. capitol
30. there
31. prophecy
32. excess
33. casual
34. compliment
35. site

CHAPTER 10   DOUBLING THE FINAL CONSONANT

PRETEST

Chagrimed

1. planner
2. witty
3. streaked
4. plugger
5. taxing
6. exploiter
7. dropped
8. beginning
9. occurrence
10. dimly
11. repealed
12. transferring
13. propellant
14. gossipy
15. instilling
16. equipped
17. omitted
18. dimmer
19. excellent
20. conference
21. benefited
22. chagrined
23. vexing
24. delightful
25. trafficker

TRAFFICKER
delightful

If you had 22 of 25 correct you may bypass this chapter. But before you do, find your wrong answers (if any) below, and read the corresponding frames in the chapter so that you will not misspell any words in this test.

TRAFFicker   *TRAFFicker*

Answer numbers	Frames	Answer numbers	Frames
1, 2, 3, 4, 5, 7, 10, 18, 23	1–4	12	14
		22	18–20
6, 8, 9, 11, 13, 14, 15, 17, 21, 24	10–11	19, 20	21–27
		25	28–29
16	12		

panicky TRAFFick

POSTTEST

1. reference
2. allotter
3. controlling
4. galloped
5. preferring
6. excellence
7. frolicsome
8. beginning
9. conference
10. mimicking
11. referred
12. rebellion
13. chagrining
14. panicky
15. visitor
16. occurrence

17. skimming	20. equipped	23. transferring
18. mimicry	21. relaxed	24. deference
19. difference	22. existence	25. concealed

For any wrong answer(s) check the frame references below and reread that part of the program. You do not want to leave this chapter without spelling every word in the test correctly.

Answer numbers	Frames	Answer numbers	Frames
17	1–4	13	18–20
2, 3, 4, 5, 8, 11, 12,	10–11	1, 6, 9, 24	21–27
15, 16, 19, 21, 22, 25		7, 10, 14, 18	28–29
20	12		
23	14		

CHAPTER 11   THE FINAL *E*

PRETEST *desiring*

1. desiring	9. argument	17. singeing	25. indispensable
2. useless	10. writing	18. manageable	26. ninth
3. serviceable	11. truly	19. arguing	27. writing
4. duly	12. changeable	20. adventuresome	28. management
5. density	13. wholesome	21. diner	29. accurately
6. advantageous	14. advertisement	22. canoeist	30. dyeing
7. coming	15. losing	23. enforceable	
8. receivable	16. rarity	24. wholly	

If you had 27 of 30 correct, you may bypass this chapter. But before you do, find your wrong answer numbers (if any) below, and read the corresponding frames in the chapter so that you will not misspell any words in this test.

Answer numbers	Frames	Answer numbers	Frames
1, 5, 7, 10, 15, 16,	1–6	26	15–17
21, 25, 27		9, 19	18–20
3, 6, 8, 12, 18, 23,	7–11	22	22–25
28		17, 30	26–27
2, 13, 14, 20, 29	12–14	4, 11, 24	28–30

POSTTEST

1. achievement	9. judging	17. receiving	25. rarity
2. advisable	10. remoteness	18. density	26. achieving
3. canoeing	11. truly	19. pursuer	27. imaginable
4. pleasurable	12. trueness	20. wholly	28. hoeing
5. manageable	13. singeing	21. changeable	29. argument
6. ageless	14. disadvantaged	22. aching	30. pronounceable
7. canoeist	15. arguing	23. desirous	
8. noticeable	16. hopeless	24. advantageous	

For any wrong answer(s) check the frame references below and reread that part of the program. You do not want to leave this chapter without spelling every word in the test correctly.

Answer numbers	Frames	Answer numbers	Frames
2, 4, 9, 14, 17, 18,	1–6	15, 29	18–20
19, 22, 23, 25, 26,		3, 7, 28	22–25
27		13	26–27
5, 8, 21, 24, 30	7–11	11, 20	28–30
1, 6, 10, 12, 16	12–14		

CHAPTER 12   THE FINAL Y

PRETEST

1. accompaniment
2. conveys
3. occupying
4. copyist
5. stories
6. burial
7. beauties
8. employer

9. tries
10. tragedies
11. applying
12. happily
13. carrying
14. hungrily
15. beautiful
16. dormitories

17. happiness
18. daily
19. studying
20. pitiful
21. displaying
22. companies
23. pitying
24. cozily

25. chimneys
26. societies
27. trial
28. theories
29. accompanied
30. industries

If you had 27 of 30 correct, you may bypass this chapter. But before you do, find your wrong answer numbers (if any) below, and read the corresponding frames in the chapter so that you will not misspell any words in this test.

Answer numbers	Frames	Answer numbers	Frames
2, 8, 21, 25	1–4	18	8–13
1, 3, 4, 5, 6, 7, 9, 10, 11, 12, 13, 14, 15, 16, 17, 19, 20, 22, 23, 24, 26, 27, 28, 29, 30	5–7		

POSTTEST

1. summaries
2. annoyance
3. copier
4. relies
5. portrays
6. defying
7. burial
8. daily

9. paid
10. monkeys
11. societies
12. employed
13. lobbying
14. medleys
15. cemeteries
16. tendencies

17. accompaniment
18. keyed
19. trying
20. laid
21. copyist
22. universities
23. controversies
24. pitiless

25. readying
26. denial
27. luxuries
28. employment
29. said
30. academies

For any wrong answer(s) check the frame references below and reread that part of the program. You do not want to leave this chapter without spelling every word in the test correctly.

Answer numbers	Frames	Answer numbers	Frames
2, 5, 10, 12, 14, 18, 28	1–4	8, 9, 20, 29	8–13
1, 3, 4, 6, 7, 11, 13, 15, 16, 17, 19, 21, 22, 23, 24, 25, 26, 27, 30	5–7		

CHAPTER 13   *IE* OR *EI*

PRETEST

1. relieve
2. conceit
3. receive
4. seizure

5. deficient
6. weighed
7. chief
8. piece

9. weird
10. counterfeit
11. height   weight
12. achieve

13. foreign
14. neighborhood
15. leisure

If you had 13 of 15 correct, you may bypass this chapter. But before you do, find your wrong answer numbers (if any) below, and read the corresponding frames in the chapter so that you will not misspell any words in this test.

Answer numbers	Frames	Answer numbers	Frames
1, 2, 3, 7, 8, 12	1–7	11	22–25
4, 9, 15	8–11	10, 13	27–35
6, 11, 14	14–21	5	39–47

POSTTEST

1. believe	5. receive	9. yield	13. thief
2. siege	6. forfeit	10. seize	14. leisure
3. sovereign	7. reindeer	11. weigh	15. weird
4. freight	8. efficient	12. deficient	

For any wrong answer(s) check the frame references below and reread that part of the program. You do not want to leave this chapter without spelling every word in the test correctly.

Answer numbers	Frames	Answer numbers	Frames
1, 2, 5, 9, 13	1–7	3, 6	27–35
10, 14, 15	8–11	8, 12	39–47
4, 7, 11	14–21		

CHAPTER 14   PLURALS

PRETEST

1. displays	9. Negroes	17. universities	25. data
2. penalties	10. melodies	18. Tories	26. heroes
3. gases	11. perches	19. discrepancies	27. wives
4. vetoes	12. thieves	20. griefs	28. studies
5. zoos	13. potatoes	21. halves	29. decoys
6. monarchs	14. Tommys	22. societies	30. taxes
7. inquiries	15. wishes	23. gulfs	
8. crises	16. buzzes	24. elegies	

If you had 27 of 30 correct, you may bypass this chapter. But before you do, find your wrong answer numbers (if any) below, and read the corresponding frames in the chapter so that you will not misspell any words in this test.

Answer numbers	Frames	Answer numbers	Frames
3, 6, 11, 15, 16, 23, 30	1–6	4, 5, 9, 13, 26	19–22
		12, 20, 21	24–26
1, 2, 7, 10, 17, 19, 22, 24, 28, 29	7–8	27	27–28
		8, 25	31–32
14, 18	9–10		

POSTTEST

1. lives	9. shelves	17. bungalows	25. Henrys
2. switches	10. addenda	18. compresses	26. epochs
3. monarchs	11. photos	19. crises	27. Negroes
4. echoes	12. treaties	20. fashions	28. hypotheses
5. analyses	13. tomatoes	21. data	29. lobbies
6. gulches	14. media	22. knives	30. wolves
7. stereos	15. Kennedys	23. deputies	
8. countries	16. companies	24. families	

For any wrong answer(s) check the frame references below and reread that part of the program. You do not want to leave this chapter without spelling every word in the test correctly.

Answer numbers	Frames		Answer numbers	Frames
2, 3, 6, 17, 18, 20, 26	1–6		9, 30	24–26
			1, 22	27–28
8, 12, 16, 23, 24, 29	7–8		5, 10, 14, 19, 21, 28	31–32
15, 25	9–10			
4, 7, 11, 13, 27	19–22			

CHAPTER 15   POSSESSIVES

PRETEST
1. king's
2. boys'
3. Brannon and Butterworth's
4. John Donne's
5. secretary's and treasurer's
6. women's
7. each other's
8. Louis the Thirteenth's
9. its
10. nobody's
11. friend's
12. father-in-law's
13. minute's

If you had 11 of 13 correct, you may bypass this chapter. But before you do, find your wrong answer numbers (if any) below, and read the corresponding frames in the chapter so that you will not misspell any words in this test.

Answer numbers	Frames		Answer numbers	Frames
1, 2, 4, 6, 11, 13	1–4		3, 5, 8, 12	8–9
7, 9, 10	5–7			

POSTTEST
1. hers
2. others'
3. niece's
4. anyone's
5. sopranos'
6. Day and May's
7. sisters'
8. theirs
9. its
10. runner-up's
11. actresses'
12. men's
13. **Lucy's**
14. brother-in-law's
15. Jack's and Jim's

For any wrong answer(s) check the frame references below and reread that part of the program. You do not want to leave this chapter without spelling every word in the test correctly.

Answer numbers	Frames		Answer numbers	Frames
3, 5, 7, 11, 12, 13	1–4		6, 10, 14, 15	3–9
1, 2, 4, 8, 9	5–7			

CHAPTER 16   LY AND OUS

PRETEST
A. *ly-ally*

1. basically	6. publicly	11. finally	16. coyly
2. morally	7. accidentally	12. accurately	17. dryly or drily
3. truly	8. angrily	13. vaguely	18. safely
4. frequently	9. chiefly	14. wholly	19. simply
5. continuously	10. duly	15. easily	20. slyly

B. *ous*

21. various	24. mischievous	27. mountainous	30. grievous
22. perilous	25. libelous	28. adventurous	31. victorious
23. advantageous	26. piteous	29. troublous	32. spacious

If you had 18 of 20 in A and 10 of 12 in B correct, you may bypass this chapter. But before you do, find your wrong answer numbers (if any) below, and read the corresponding frames in the chapter so that you will not misspell any words in this test.

Answer numbers	Frames	Answer numbers	Frames
A.		B.	
2, 4, 5, 7, 9, 11	1–3	22, 24, 25, 27, 30	22–23
3, 10, 12, 13, 14,	4–6	23, 28, 29, 32	24–25
18, 19		21, 26, 31	26–29
8, 15, 16, 17, 20	7–10		
1, 6	15		

POSTTEST

A. *ly-ally*

1. really	6. finally	11. academically	16. perceptibly
2. angrily	7. publicly	12. entirely	17. drastically
3. truly	8. hungrily	13. simply	18. duly
4. shyly or shily	9. apologetically	14. likely	19. trickily
5. certainly	10. wholly	15. tastily	20. slyly

B. *ous*

21. grievous	24. courageous	27. ridiculous	20. riotous
22. desirous	25. gracious	28. bounteous	31. injurious
23. hazardous	26. plenteous	29. dangerous	32. mischievous

For any wrong answer(s) check the frame references below and reread that part of the program. You do not want to leave this chapter without spelling every word in the test correctly.

Answer numbers	Frames	Answer numbers	Frames
A.		B.	
1, 5, 6	1–3	21, 23, 29, 30, 32	22–23
3, 10, 12, 13, 14	4–6	22, 24, 25, 27	24–25
18		26, 28, 31	26–29
2, 4, 8, 15, 19, 20	7–10		
16	12–14		
7, 9, 11, 17	15–16		

TEST   PART THREE

A.

1. F	6. T	11. F	16. F
2. F	7. F	12. F	17. T
3. T	8. T	13. T	18. T
4. F	9. T	14. T	19. T
5. T	10. F	15. T	20. T

B.

21. grimmer
22. dropping
23. equipped
24. beginning
25. occurrence
26. preference
27. losing
28. rudeness
29. desirous
30. portrayal
31. receivable
32. envoys
33. discrepancies
34. denial
35. Kennedys
36. difference
37. publicly
38. critically
39. reliably
40. hungrily
41. excellency
42. chagrining
43. controlled
44. managing
45. serviceable
46. immensity
47. argument
48. arguing
49. societies
50. tries
51. mimicry
52. equipage
53. gossipy
54. usage
55. frolicsome

FINAL TEST

A.

1. in can ta tion
2. com men da tion
3. aus pi cious
4. math e mat i cal
5. ac cu mu late
6. har ass ment
7. ser vi tude
8. in cal cu la ble
9. bi og ra phy
10. com mem o ra tion

B.

11. expelling
12. transferred
13. rebuttal
14. benefited
15. gripper
16. portraiture
17. laid
18. dyeing
19. copying
20. wholly
21. steadying
22. canoeist
23. recurring
24. ninth
25. becoming
26. argument
27. thornier
28. divinity
29. panicky
30. stinginess

C.

31. foreign
32. thieves
33. forfeit
34. seized
35. weird
36. reins
37. conscientious
38. receive
39. mischievous
40. Ancient

D.

41. except
42. thorough
43. then
44. quite
45. consul
46. access
47. lose
48. capital
49. principal
    effect
50. passed
51. causal
52. personnel
53. cite
54. advice
55. all right

E.

56. recede
57. accede
58. supersede
59. exceed
60. concede
61. intercede
62. proceed
63. precede
64. succeed
65. antecede

F.

66. performs
67. description
68. C
69. perspires
70. dissolved
71. C
72. C
73. misstatement
74. recommend
75. procedure
76. dissent
77. C
78. C
79. disservice
80. C

G.

81. publicly
82. plenteous
83. truly
84. piteous
85. courageous
86. dryly, drily
87. conceivably
88. continuous
89. angrily
90. spacious
91. duly
92. various
93. slyly
94. advantageous
95. wholly

H.

96. heroes
97. potatoes
98. Negroes
99. tragedies
100. replies
101. its
102. bullies
103. vetoes
104. thieves
105. everybody's
106. society's
107. cries
108. lives
109. mother's
110. day's

I.

111. hindrance
112. occasionally
113. recognize
114. financier
115. parallel
116. humorous
117. privilege
118. peculiar
119. environment
120. ridiculous
121. familiar
122. dormitory
123. lightning
124. tragedy
125. disastrous

J.

126. evitable
127. prominence
128. surprise
129. noticeable
130. digestible
131. significant
132. defendant
133. analyze
134. advertise
135. stationary
136. experience
137. rectifiable
138. persistent
139. assistant
140. insistent
141. supervise
142. exercise
143. perceptible
144. pitiable
145. abundance

K.

146. debt
147. loneliness
148. acquire
149. acclaim
150. procedure
151. accommodate
152. controversy
153. aggravate
154. mathematics
155. similar
156. appall
157. sentence
158. benefit
159. acquaint
160. government
161. athlete
162. liable
163. occasionally
164. category
165. grammar
166. comparative
167. quantity
168. background
169. assemble
170. bulletin

APPENDIX A GUIDELINES FOR SYLLABICATION

PRETEST

1. nec es sar y
2. man u fac ture
3. vow el
4. ac com mo date
5. car pen ter
6. rap id
7. con sid er a tion
8. an tip a thy
9. ge ol o gy
10. rub ble
11. ref er ence
12. ac cu mu late
13. de lude
14. pi lot
15. soph o more
16. an ti bod y
17. con so nant
18. ap pear ance
19. trib u la tion
20. ri val ry

If you had 18 of 20 correct, you may bypass this section.

POSTTEST

1. con tro ver sy
2. res tau rant
3. re cur rence
4. pre cede
5. dis ap point ment
6. tre men dous
7. un nec es sar y
8. de scrip tion
9. op por tu ni ty
10. ad van tage ous
11. in ci den tal
12. doc u men ta ry

13. knowl   edge
14. Wed   nes   day
15. psy   chol   o   gy
16. ri   dic   u   lous

17. a   chieve   ment
18. for   got   ten
19. gov   ern   ment
20. pro   ce   dure

If you missed any, reread frames 13–24 and 30–34 so that you will not leave this part of the program without dividing every word in the test correctly.

Index

Index